The Paper Cut-Out Design Book

The Paper Cut-Out Design Book

*A sourcebook for creating and adapting
the heritage of American Folk Art, Polish Wycinanki,
Chinese Hua Yang, Japanese Kirigami,
German Scherenschnitte and others*

by Ramona Jablonski

1976

STEMMER
HOUSE
PUBLISHERS, INC.

Owings Mills, Maryland

The quotation on page 99 is from *An Invitation to See:
125 Paintings from the Museum of Modern Art* by Helen M.
Franc. Copyright © 1973 The Museum of Modern Art,
New York. All rights reserved. Reprinted by permission of
The Museum of Modern Art.

The compositional and instructional photographs throughout
the book are by Charles L. Smith. The instructional drawings
are by Gerard A. Valerio.

Inquiries are to be directed to
STEMMER HOUSE PUBLISHERS, INC.
2627 Caves Road, Owings Mills,
Maryland 21117

A BARBARA HOLDRIDGE BOOK

Printed and bound in the United States of America

First Edition

Library of Congress Cataloging in Publication Data
Jablonski, Romona, 1939-
The paper cut-out design book.
1. Paper work. I. Title.
TT870.J3   736'.98   76-2467
ISBN 0-916144-03-8
ISBN 0-916144-04-6

Contents

Introduction

I am Polish by marriage. My college work and professional background are in the art field. Exposure to the Polish culture brought the folk art of paper-cutting to my attention. I've not been the same since.

Research into "Wycinanki" (Polish paper cut-out design) was difficult. Written material in English was almost non-existent. But research did bring to light the fact that paper-cutting as an art form is not limited to Poland. Indeed, it stretches back into antiquity and is present in one form or another in almost every culture. Therefore we Americans are heirs to a rich artistic heritage through our varied ethnic cultures. Most familiar, perhaps, is the German tradition in design, which comes down to us through the Pennsylvania German cultural group. However, the Chinese, Japanese, Mexican, Swiss, Polish and other cultures all add to our heritage. What I have done here is to gather together in one book the information collected from many sources over a period of years, so that this lovely art form can be learned, practiced, enjoyed and perpetuated.

The materials are simple: paper, scissors and paste. Subject matter is all around us: pots on a window sill, architectural detail, the paper on the wall, the rugs on the floor, a sketch in an advertisement, a scene remembered from childhood. The cutting technique can range from bold slashes to intricate snipping. It is therefore adaptable to the capabilities of children wishing to make snowflakes at Christmas, or to the abilities of senior citizens whose wealth of experience can provide a treasure of subject matter. Artists in other media may find inspiration and new directions for their own work through paper-cut designs.

The creative possibilities of paper-cutting are limitless. If you were learning to paint, you would use the paint, brushes and canvas to produce your own very personal result—your own style. With paper-cutting, the same is true—you use scissors and paper, and the end result as you have pasted it down is uniquely your own. After all, paper-cutting is a folk art. As such it is constantly evolving. You and I are just as folksy as anyone and so there is sound historic reason for us to share in the evolution of this art in any way we see fit.

So use this book as inspiration and as an instructor literally at your hand. Study the "old country" examples to learn the techniques. Copy some examples to help the learning process. Look at others for their wealth of creative source material. Then take off on your own paper wings!

RAMONA JABLONSKI

Baltimore, Maryland
April, 1976

Appreciation

So many people have given so enthusiastically of their time, talent, knowledge and encouragement to make this book possible that it is difficult to thank them all. A partial list would include Mary Hammond Sullivan, Marie Edmonston, Mr. and Mrs. Charles D. Curran, Carol Lynch Perry, Beth Kidder, Mary Prince, Mr. and Mrs. John A. Schapiro, Mr. and Mrs. Harold A. Beatty, Joe Koscinski and Steve Whatley, and especially the people in the ethnic communities who have quietly kept the art of paper-cutting alive.

Thanks also must go to Barbara Holdridge, whose insight and calm leadership gave this book its form, and to Mark Haller for hours and hours of work. And most especially to Richard, for being there through it all.

The Paper Cut-Out Design Book

Cuttings from modern China—landscape, Happy Flower and flying goddess.

2

The History and the Heritage

Ever since paper was invented in 105 A.D. by Ts'ai Lun, an official in the court of Ho Ti, emperor of Cathay, paper-cutting has been a folk art. Perhaps it flowered because paper became so inexpensive and universally available, so easily workable with common tools, and so adaptable to manifold uses. Whatever the reason, it was the common folk who first learned to cut the paper, and then perpetuated these rich traditions.

The humble nature of its origins and the anonymity of its practice have caused paper-cutting to remain virtually ignored as an art form. Certainly most paper-cut work was never so much as attributed, much less signed. Ofter the paper design was only an intermediate step in the production of another art form more highly prized. One of the original uses of cut-paper designs in China was in the production of embroidery patterns, since at the time of the invention of paper, Chinese embroidery had already reached a very high state of artistry.

But no longer is paper-cutting an unappreciated Cinderella of the arts. While the materials remain simple and easily available, artists, craftspeople, collectors and even governments are becoming increasingly aware of this valuable folk heritage, and are taking steps to see that it is preserved and perpetuated.

The Chinese Heritage

Paper-cuttings have been made in China for at least fifteen centuries. We know this because paper-cuttings were among the archaeological finds at Kaochang (in the Sinkiang Uighur region) excavated in 1959; and objects from that excavation are dated between 514 and 551 A.D. The degree of skill evident in the cut-paper horses and monkeys indicates that the art form had already achieved a high level at that time.

Writings from the T'ang and Sung dynasties indicate that paper-cut decorations were used by rich and poor alike. Part of any girl's preparation for marriage included training in paper-cutting, as well as in embroidery; and on her wedding day, these two skills were deemed the criteria of the bride's accomplishments and intelligence.

At the time of the annual Spring Festival, folk arts in general and paper-cutting in particular really had a chance for special glory. That was (and is) the time of year when "out with the old and in with the new" became the rule of the season. Debts were paid and houses were cleaned. Paper-cuttings were used as interior and exterior decorations.

Hua Yang design of kissing birds.

Paper on the walls and windowpanes was removed and replaced. The gaily colored cut-outs named Window Flowers were pasted on windowpanes. Ceiling Flowers were used as ceiling decorations, and columns and lintels were decorated with Luck Hangings. Doors and walls all shared in the renewal, to stay resplendent until just before the next Spring Festival. Smaller and less permanent paper-cuttings called Happy Flowers were pasted on mirrors, lanterns and gifts, and even used as decorations on cakes. And to this day Spring Festival is the time when women shop for new cut-paper embroidery patterns ("Hua Yang") to be tacked or glued on hats, aprons and slippers, and then covered with row after row of bright floss.

If you had been a member of the nobility during the T'ang dynasty, you might well have been invited to the Emperor's Court to share in the festivities. As an opening favor you might have received a silk flag decorated with gold and silver cut-paper designs in the form of spring flowers and lettering. Smaller spring flags were used to festoon the garden bushes and to pin in ladies' hair—and sometimes, when everyone was overcome by the mood of the season, in men's hair as well. Later, after being given a gift of a paper flower, you might have been expected to compose a poem.

And now it is time to get back to the plain folk . . .

While the Spring Festival was the major showplace for the paper-cutter's art, there was other work throughout the year. In a Chinese funeral, cut-paper symbols were used extensively. Along with paper clothing and shoes, messages and symbols of paper might be made and burnt as gifts to accompany the dead in the other life. Birthdays and weddings must always be accompanied by appropriate wishes for good will, luck and long life—all cut from paper. Itinerant craftsmen supplied these needs. Known as the "pilgrims of the rivers and lakes," they traveled over the countryside selling their paper-cuttings to provide themselves a meager existence. While their work enjoyed tremendous popularity, these workers were accorded no status whatsoever.

Some of the ancient cuttings came from "factories" composed of a single peasant family, whose members worked on an assembly-line arrangement to supplement their farm income. One member might cut the original design, another would use it as a pattern to produce replicates, and a third member might apply the color. These paper-cuttings then were sold in an open market.

Soon, symbols became highly important in Chinese paper cut-outs. Hundreds sprang from mythology, drama or someone's fertile imagination. These quickly caught on and became recognizable throughout China. For instance, a mythical animal, Chi-lin, was thought to bring children; peach, pine and crane suggested longevity; dragons, lions and tigers symbolized courage and strength; serpent, as might be guessed, was the villain representing cunning and evil power of supernatural origin.

Once a pleasing paper-cut design was produced, it was often passed from generation to generation, and eventually was adopted by a whole region, so that there developed a certain "look" or style of cutting peculiar to that region. Flower patterns are identified with central China—not surprising, since this is also the region in which the magnificent floral silks, brocades and embroideries have been produced since ancient times.

The comparatively dry climate of the north region gave rise to the lovely Window Flowers. Here the people could use a tough but transparent paper called "Kao-li" to make their windowpanes and decorations.

Chrysanthemum — the Happy Flower

Chrysanthemums from Wang Chow City, perhaps inspired by Chang Yung-Sho.

The home of the Happy Flower is the south of China. Boldness and excellent composition mark these works native to the area around Nanking. Beautifully composed within square, rectangular, oval or diamond-shapes, the subject matter is usually presented in a few quick lines and broad planes. Especially known for their precise craftsmanship are the paper-cutters from Wenchow in Chekiang Province. Their delicate tracery work requires extreme skill and is probably among the most intricate paper-cut work in existence.

Chang Yung-Sho became a living legend in this area. Born to a humble family, he began cutting at the age of twelve. In spite of hunger and deprivation, he studied what he saw in nature around him, and learned to create from it. He is credited with creating ten thousand new designs, and is said to have been able to cut one hundred and twenty different species of chrysanthemum alone!

Chinese theatrical characters.

The Farmer Artist

Probably the best-known recent cutter from northern China is Wang Lao-Shan (1890-1951). A peasant trained in paper-cutting from early childhood, he was coloring Window Flowers at the age of seven and producing his own work by the age of twelve. A passionate fan of Peking Opera, Wang Lao-Shan is credited with producing over two hundred groups of theatrical characters as well as two hundred groups of flower and bird patterns —all within a fifty-year period. And he accomplished all of this without neglecting his daily farm work! Wang conceived art as more than simply a way to make a living; he viewed it as communication between the artist and his clients, and also among fellow artists. This exchange of ideas, he felt, was essential to the development of any art form. The insight and understanding he brought to the characters he portrayed make his work a model for the modern paper-cutters of China.

The district of Wei in Hopei Province is widely known for its cut-work, the subject matter of which is often taken from Chinese opera. Traditional theatrical figures are carved with a knife from very thin white paper (usually several layers at once), then are brightly colored with dyes.

The northwest provinces were also the home of other paper-cuttings which revealed a great strength and power of imagination. They have provided inspiration to woodcut artists as well as to paper-cutters working today. One group called New Creation, apparently sponsored by the government, excels in paper-cuttings of busy children engaged with great enthusiasm in some activity. They may be doing a lantern dance, flying a kite, sweeping the floor while mother is busy with the baby, or—not so happily, perhaps—trudging to school. The themes are aimed at encouraging modern youngsters to become industrious, contributing members of the community.

Other modern artists of this area stand out for their individuality. Chen Pin Hsing and Hsin Chai Shen used very thin lines in their dramatic scenes. Chian Ken Ho is famous for her scenes and narratives from well-loved dramas. It is reported that she could visit the theatre, remember the characters by heart and then cut them directly, without sketches. She used thick lines and bold patterns and invented her own style of composition to tell the stories, cutting with scissors rather than with the more common knife.

Boys flying kites, from the work of Hsin Chai Shen.

Traditional and Modern Techniques

Each culture in which paper-cutting has survived seems to have its own favorite paper types, colors, motifs and techniques. In the Chinese tradition, red is the most celebrated color. Used in homes and in temples, red symbolizes everything positive: grandeur, dignity, royalty, youth, beauty, courage, joy. If a paper-cutting is going to be a single color, red is a likely choice.

The professional Chinese cutter relied mostly on his assortment of knives, punches and other hand tools made by him or else to his specifications. One suggestion for making a knife reads like this: "Cut a piece off a discarded clock spring, insert it between strips of bamboo (or pliant wood) for a handle and bind together with wire. Sharpen the steel piece into a pointed blade."*

Of course, all tools must be kept extremely sharp. Even today the old-timers say, "If you want to know how good a craftsman is, look at his tools."

The paper used by the professionals is very thin, finely grained and unsized. When fewer than twenty layers are used, the packet is sewn together with needle and thread before cutting. If more copies are needed, the stack is placed inside a specially built frame, and nailed down to a base coated with a vegetable-oil-and-resin mixture to provide a flexible surface for cutting. If a pattern is being used, it is put on top of the stack. The cutting begins with the small details first, then gradually proceeds to the larger shapes. The outline is cut last. Sometimes a combination of knife-cutting and scissor-cutting is employed. The intricate part of the design can be cut most successfully with knives, gouges or a punch. Then the larger cuts and the outline are made with scissors.

Coloring is the final step. The whole bundle is colored at once. Since the paper is unsized, dyes applied to the top layer quickly soak down

* "The Art of the Paper" by Chan Feng-Kao, *China Reconstructs*, December, 1973.

through the entire stack. The dyes most commonly used are aniline, cinnabar and lazulite; they vary, however, from artist to artist.

When all of the coloring has dried, the work is ready for sale. The stacks are usually not separated until a customer has decided to buy.

When an existing cutting is to be used for a pattern, a time-honored smoking technique is used to transfer the pattern to the new paper. First a clean piece of paper is laid on a wooden board. The paper-cutting is placed on top, and the whole is then sprinkled with water and carefully smoothed out. The water causes the two layers of paper to stick together and to the board. The board is then held upside down over an oil lamp or a lamp with a paper wick. The soot from the lamp flame coats the entire surface of the paper, the heat causes the old pattern to dry quickly, and it can be peeled off, leaving a white print on the paper underneath. Of course, such interesting processes often give way to modernization, and nowadays many cutters work from printed patterns.

Through government sponsorship, paper-cutting in China has been perpetuated and revitalized. Today it is a thriving art form. Designs for book covers and illustrations, headings for newspapers, stamps and even animated films are all fertile fields for the paper-cutter's art. Much work is being done for export, and often can be found in this country in museum shops as well as in import stores featuring Chinese goods.

The paper-cutter's art at its most intricate: this fish-and-squirrel pattern was cut in Chekiang.

The Japanese Tradition: Mon-Kiri or Kirigami

The Japanese imperial crest.

The old Japanese term for paper-cutting is "Mon-kiri," which, literally translated, means "crest-cutting." The Japanese used paper-cut designs as far back as the eleventh century, as a means of creating a family emblem or crest. These crests originally appeared as textile designs displayed on the most formal costumes of high-ranking courtiers, as distinctive marks of recognition when at the Imperial court. The ruling Fujiwara family of that time encouraged the practice of using a symbol for each family name. Such emblems soon spread from formal court wear to use on carriages and costumes of all the family members when at court. Etiquette decreed that one crest appear on the center back, one on the back of each sleeve and, if one were to be really proper, one each on the right and left front of the most formal kimono. The emblems were elegantly simple in design, and featured familiar objects with which each family could be identified—flowers, cranes, musical instruments and the like.

The Samurai or warrior class took over the country at the end of the twelfth century, bringing the elegant Heian Period to an end. The military people, realizing their lack of culture, copied what they admired about their predecessors, including the use of the family crest. Crests not only made the Samurai appear more cultivated, but also served a military purpose since they were an easily recognizable symbol to take into battle on banners and weapons, and served to identify camps and headquarters. In practice, a warrior and his family would establish a crest design, and thereafter each of the family retainers employed a variation of it. In common with the previous ruling classes, the Samurai adopted symbols from their daily lives. Familiar objects—arrows, folding fans, dragonflies, hoes —were likely to be used as elements of the design.

These warrior emblems reached their highest development during the Muromachi period of the fifteenth century, when wars occurred frequently. In the Edo period of the early seventeenth century, as the Tokugawa entrenched themselves firmly enough to maintain peace, family crests returned to purely decorative use in formal costumes. Flashy, oddly shaped emblems fell into disfavor, and simpler, more refined symbols appeared, usually in a circular motif. Common people began cutting crests to enhance the beauty of their own kimonos; embroidered crests on articles other than clothing also came into vogue. As before, subjects were drawn from everyday life—snowflakes, animals, spools, tools, mountains, sailboats and the like. Some motifs borrowed from the Ming dynasty in China—shells, dragons and clouds, bats, balance weights and others—were employed as well.

It has been estimated that there are between three and five hundred family crests in existence in Japan. If variations are counted, the number increases to several thousand. Most of them have fallen into disuse, but a few remain familiar today. The most conspicuous is the sixteen-petal chrysanthemum, the emblem of the Imperial family, created in the Meiji period (1868-1912). Throughout that time it was forbidden for anyone else to use a chrysanthemum in any form as part of a crest.

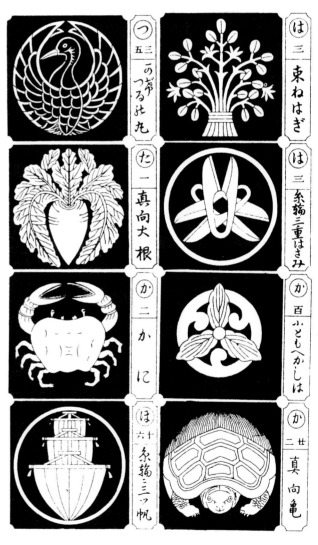

Some of these Japanese family crests may have originated from paper-cuttings. All of them, however, can serve as inspiration for cutters of today.

9

An intricately cut Japanese paper stencil, from the
collection of Carol Lynch Perry.

Inevitably, the modern development of the crest has expanded to include the establishment of trademarks for organizations and corporations. While the old family crests are still worn occasionally, they are more for decoration than identity.

Mon-kiri designs are usually cut from squares of paper, which may be folded up to six times. The cutting is done with scissors. Of course, whatever design is cut into the folded paper packet is multiplied by the number of layers of paper. Thus, something that may look very simple in the folded and cut stage becomes an intricate and complicated creation when fully opened.

Paper-cutting is learned early in Japan's schools, where the traditional admiration of artistic accomplishment is combined with respect for the nation's cultural heritage. History and art blend delightfully for a child learning to cut the crests of those warriors of old—or perhaps even inventing a crest of his own!

With the expansion of the art of paper-cutting into areas beyond the traditional Mon-kiri or crest-cutting, a more general name has been devised. It is "Kirigami," derived from "kiri," meaning cutting, and "gami," meaning paper.

Another outstanding application of the Japanese craftsman's ability is the cutting of stencils. Stenciling is a very old means of applying color and pattern to fabrics. It involves cutting holes in a masking material—in this case it is paper—then laying that mask (or stencil) on a length of fabric and brushing pigment (usually dye) through the holes so that when the stencil is removed a design remains on the fabric. The stencil is then moved to a fresh location on the fabric, carefully aligned or "registered" with the first stenciled impression, and the dye brushed on again. This process is repeated for the length and width of the fabric until it is completely covered with the stenciled design. A second stencil can be made to complement the design of the first, and a second color applied to the fabric after the first color has set. Then a third stencil can be made for a third color, and so on.

Sometimes instead of stenciling a length of fabric to be sewn into a garment, the garment is made first and the stencil then designed to enhance the lines of it. This method works particularly well on the Japanese kimono, a beautifully simple piece of clothing which can be laid out absolutely flat and then worked on.

By using stencils, the Japanese craftsman enjoyed much more freedom of design than his western counterpart. The westerner worked within the limitations of printing blocks or rollers; he could lay down blocks of color only in flat, even tones. The stenciler could start with his pigment heavy at the top of the stencil and fade it to almost nothing at the bottom if he wished. He could mix colors or blend them on the same stencil. Or he could change colors completely each time he repositioned the stencil.

When we think of clothing here in the West, we usually consider the style of the garment, as well as the design on the fabric. In Japan the kimono style was set centuries ago by custom and practicality. With style predetermined, the design on the kimono becomes the prominent means of individual expression. A dyer using paper-cut stencils could meet the most individual requirements of the designer.

The paper stencil plate was introduced into Japan by a dyer named Someya Yuzen toward the end of the seventeenth century. It is not clear where he came from, but the production of the cut-paper stencil is tanta-

lizingly reminiscent of Chinese paper-cutting methods. One feature showed a touch of pure Japanese thrift, however—their stencils were cut from old unused documents! Recycling isn't such a new idea.

The Chinese methods served the Japanese well, especially when it came to making reinforced stencils. A paper stencil, of course, is fragile, especially when saturated with wet dye. Japanese ingenuity overcame the problem. Using a tough paper made of mulberry fiber and persimmon juice, waterproofed with a hard-drying oil, the cutter would tack together six or more sheets. His pattern was either an old stencil or a new sketch; his tool a long, thin, extremely sharp knife, which was pushed rather than pulled to cut the design. Important to the end result were the small holes punched in the corners as "register marks" so that the stencils could be properly aligned during the dying process.

After the design had been completely cut, two of the copies were dampened with water to insure that they would expand equally when wet, and contract equally when dry. One of the wet sheets was laid down flat and coated with an adhesive. Then, silk threads (or in some cases, human hairs) were stretched across it at regular intervals in a grid pattern. The ends were allowed to hang out into the margin. The second wet sheet then was carefully placed on top of the threads and aligned by means of the register marks. The whole was carefully pressed together and allowed to dry. From the original stack of six copies, two more stencils could be made in an identical fashion. Stencils made by this process had the strength of the double thickness of paper, plus the reinforcement of the silk threads which were so fine that they left no trace on the finished fabric.

The subject matter of the Japanese stenciler knew no limits. If it could be written or drawn, it could be cut. Even love letters have shown up in stencil form! The Japanese cutter was, perhaps, inspired more by nature and less by mythology and drama than his Chinese counterpart.

Paper-cut stencils were also employed in the production of the traditional Japanese hanging pictures (kakemonos), although to a much lesser extent. Through a clever combination of stenciling and hand-blending of colors, the artist could produce pictures hardly distinguishable from water-colors.

Since stencils were originally used for decorating fabric, they were considered as a means to an end, without intrinsic value. Only in recent times have these lovely stencils been appreciated for themselves, as works of great imagination and skill.

A cut-paper stencil with thread grid for reinforcement. Courtesy of Carol Lynch Perry

This detail shows another stencil-cutting technique. "Bridges" of paper are left in to hold parts of the design together. Courtesy of Carol Lynch Perry

Courtesy of Carol Lynch Perry

11

Pennsylvania Dutch, 1840. Called a fractur (from the Latin fractura) *for its ornamented writing, an adaptation of Gothic script. Courtesy of Hallmark Cards Incorporated*

A seamstress from the whimsical world of Margareta Bredan.

The German Tradition: Scherenschnitte

In the Middle Ages, when the Church was the only stable institution left in western Europe, cloistered members of religious orders became the leading artists and craftsmen of the day. Their "Klosterarbeit" or cloister work took many forms. Medieval manuscript illumination was practiced widely and was well known. At the same time, almost as a recreational activity, religious paper-cuttings or "prayer pictures" developed. These usually featured sacred scenes or figures cut from single pieces of paper and intricately hand-painted. They were used by the monks as gifts to one another or to laymen in commemoration of religious occasions. Sometimes they were done simply as a religious exercise.

As Europe emerged from the Middle Ages, secular folk copied the idea, and German paper-cutting, "Scherenschnitte," came into its own. Godparents fashioned paper New Years wishes for their godchildren. Relatives cut decorative certificates to present to children at their confirmations. Official marriage and baptismal certificates likewise were adorned with illuminations and cuttings. Quite often, a young man planning to be married would cut an elaborate paper gift for his bride on the wedding day. And thus the art spread from the monasteries to the countryside where it became firmly entrenched as a folk art, taking many forms ranging from devout religious scenes to spritely illustrations of folk and fairy tales. For a time in the late 1700s and early 1800s, life-sized silhouette portraits cut from black paper enjoyed wide popularity.

But long before then, political turmoil had taken its toll in Germany. Prolonged wars, religious persecution and corrupt civil authority brought poverty and starvation to the peasant classes. When English shipping agents made their way down the Rhine in the late seventeenth century looking for customers to fill their ships to the New World, thousands of country folk did not need much convincing. Many had already heard the stories sent back by the first wave of German immigrants to America, about the land of religious and political freedom where there was wealth to be made in virgin territory. So they piled aboard the unsanitary ships, bringing their language and literature, attitudes and arts with them to the shores of America.

They came from the Palatinate region of Germany, from the Lower Rhine, Alsace-Lorraine, Moravia, Saxony and Switzerland. They landed in New York, New Jersey, Maryland and South Carolina. For many, the ultimate destination was Penn's colony, established so that his Quakers could enjoy religious freedom. Those who were indentured gravitated there after they had worked off their debts. Others, more fortunate, established homesteads immediately. They settled in the territory now comprising Berks, Lehigh, Lebanon, Dauphin, Lancaster and York counties in southeastern Pennsylvania—the heart of "Pennsylvania Dutch" country.

While diverse backgrounds were represented among these people (some said the German jails had been emptied, others affirmed that men of skill and letters were included), those who occupied the Pennsylvania countryside shared some things in common. Universal was the desire to be left to their own interpretation of the Bible and of what constituted a moral way of life. And they shared a common artistic background. True, the art forms they had known at a level of elegance in Europe suffered some roughening because of the realities of life on the frontier. But the heritage was there, to be drawn upon once the necessities of survival were assured and time could be found to nourish the aesthetic sense.

One of the early arts to emerge was "Frakturschrift"—the broken Gothic lettering and painting on important documents so reminiscent of old manuscript illuminations. It soon was joined by Scherenschnitte—paper-cutting—either as a further means of ornamenting documents or as an independent art form.

Courtesy of the artist, Margareta Bredan

A Pennsylvania German fold-and-cut design with hand painting. Courtesy of Hallmark Cards Incorporated

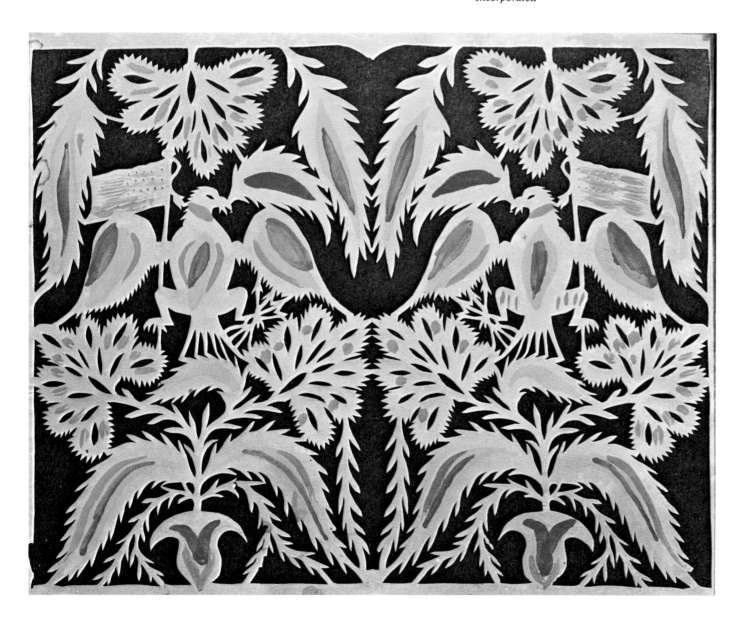

13

"Liberty," courtesy of The Henry Francis du Pont Winterthur Museum. Notice the carefully applied knife-slashed detail work.

Courtesy of the artist, Margareta Bredan

The German-style cutting was usually made from a single sheet of white paper, either cut flat or folded. Both knives and scissors were used by the men and women who practiced the craft. Many times a texture was added to parts of the finished work by stippling with pin pricks or controlled slashes of the knife point. After the basic cutting was completed, color might be added with paint created from a mixture of whisky and varnish, the latter made of cherry-tree gum diluted with water—or some other equally homespun recipe. Coloring matter could be extracted from plants or clay deposits. Or bits of colored paper or cloth might be added either atop or beneath the basic cut.

Certain motifs were repeated often and are now closely associated with the Pennsylvania Dutch tradition. Among these are the tulip, bird, heart, unicorn, mermaid and numerous animals, all important in the legend and folklore of the old country. During the fight for independence, the eagle, the thirteen-star flag and the motto "Liberty" were often used.

One of the most charming traditions was that of the "Liebesbrief" or loveletter. A young man named Johannes Uhlman popularized the form in the mid-1700s, when he cut an amazingly intricate missive from a folded square of paper. He embellished it with hearts and flowers, birds, and just about every love verse known to man, then sent it along

Pennsylvania German circular valentine, cut-out and hand colored, with sentiments of love sent to Miss Elizabeth Sandwith on the 14th of February, 1753. It must have done the trick—she later became the wife of the sender, Henry Drinker, a Pennsylvania Quaker. From the Abby Aldrich Rockefeller Folk Art Collection, Williamsburg, Virginia

with six coffee dishes to his lady love. Apparently her delight was less than permanent, because eventually the two went their separate ways. At that point scruple overcame temptation: the dishes and the letter were returned intact.

Doubtless after seeing or hearing of this work of art, every young lady in the county yearned for one. So many a young man spent many a long winter evening laboriously cutting valentines. Sometimes a cut-paper loveletter did the job of proposing for a gentleman who was too shy to speak. And of course it became a highly prized keepsake to the young lady who received it.

The Pennsylvania Germans also gave us a rich heritage of decorated furniture and accessories for the home. Many of these articles were decorated with stencils cut from paper. Unable to afford furniture either imported from Europe or fashioned by prestigious American cabinet-makers, the rural folk contented themselves with pieces made locally of pine or maple. To disguise the plain, rough quality of the wood, the householders would either paint these pieces themselves or hire itinerant craftsmen, who could and often did decorate everything from the kitchen salt box to the parlor walls and floor.

These craftsmen cut their own stencils from oiled paper. Care was taken to bevel the edges of each stencil so that the painted design would have a crisp, clear edge. Sometimes a single stencil would suffice for a complete design. Other times a set of several stencils would be needed, especially for a design in many colors.

The paint, too, was locally made, using the familiar clays and dyes, or brick dust mixed with skim milk. It was laid on flat over the stencil with a stiff, blunt brush. Yankee ingenuity and oiled stencil paper could make ordinary plaster look as fine as French wallpaper. Even the com-

Children's parade. Courtesy of the artist, Margareta Bredan

15

ponents of large murals were applied with enlarged paper stencils, then finished with touches applied freehand by the artist.

Stenciling was not confined to the Pennsylvania area but was found throughout New England, Ohio, Indiana and even further west. It had many applications, from elaborate murals and furnishings to mere artistic exercises produced by young ladies. From the close of the Revolutionary War until well into the nineteenth century, stenciling was one of the primary forms of interior decoration among the common folk of America.

Switzerland

Since paper-cutting is primarily an art form of everyday people, most pieces are unsigned. Certain Swiss cutters, however, became well known throughout Europe in the late 1800s and early 1900s; their work had such style and individuality that it was recognizable even without a signature.

One such craftsman was Johann Jakob Hauswirth (1808-1871). He took his early inspiration from crests and stenciled furniture produced in the seventeenth century. Gradually, however, his rural background won out and his work became a chronicle of country life. His distinctive

Courtesy of the artist, Walter VonGunten

Courtesy of the artist, Walter VonGunten

17

Courtesy of the artist, Walter VonGunten

trees, leaves and animals became his trademark. And his work served to inspire later artists to take up paper-cutting seriously. Louis Saugy and Christian Schwizgebel are probably the best-known among them.

Saugy, the son of an art teacher, became a devotee of paper-cutting when his duties as a mail carrier took him into homes where framed works of Hauswirth were displayed. Inspired, he began cutting seriously, and before long his skillful heart-shaped compositions, created from paper folded a single time, brought him distinction. His subject matter, like Hauswirth's, leaned to rural outdoor scenes. Later in life, he and a devoted student produced collages of great color and intricacy.

Schwizgebel's exposure to Hauswirth's work came about in the same way as Saugy's, except that instead of delivering mail, he was carrying bread from his father's bakery to Swiss homes where paper-cuttings were displayed. Deciding to try his hand, the young man produced alpine scenes which won him an art scholarship. Still, he remained obscure until an antique dealer saw his work in 1950 and asked him to do some copies of Hauswirth. Soon he was much in demand, not only for copies but for his own renderings of birth and confirmation certificates and similar work.

America is the fortunate heir to another gifted paper-cutter from Switzerland. Walter von Gunten grew up in the 1940s in a small town near Bern, Switzerland. His interest aroused by the great eighteenth-century paper-cuttings he saw in Swiss museums and galleries, he used his mother's sewing scissors to practice (just as his predecessors had) until he had taught himself the art of Scherenschnitte. He used modern as well as traditional designs.

After his work had been well received at exhibitions in several European cities, he came to America in 1961 and continuing his cutting there. As he began using indigenous plants, animals and scenes, his work began to take on American aspects. While he was able to keep the European flavor, he added more detail than the old European masters had put into their work.

Today Mr. von Gunten works from his studio in Oshkosh, Wisconsin. He never folds the paper to produce a design; rather he cuts each one from a single flat sheet, and no two are ever exactly alike. He lightly sketches the scene first, then cuts it out with tiny, super-sharp sewing scissors. A typical design will take days to complete. The cutting is then spread out and pasted to a plain background—a process so exacting that it requires hours of work, and cannot be interrupted until the entire piece is pasted.

Mr. vonGunten has shown his work in exhibits in cities all over America and has been the subject of many magazine articles and television features. He is credited with reviving the art of Scherenschnitte.

The Polish Tradition: Wycinanki

"Wycinanki" is pronounced *vee-chee-non-kee*. It is the Polish word for paper-cut designs.

   Just when and why this art form began to flower in Poland seems a matter of some uncertainty. Some say that it goes back to the time when few farmhouses had glass windows. To keep out the elements, peasant farmers hung sheep skins over the window openings. Then, to let in some light and air, they took their sheep shears and snipped small openings in the skins, and these were soon recognized as decorative as well as functional. Another source says that there came a time in the mid-nineteenth century when favorable social and economic factors allowed the peasants time and resources to develop their special genius for decoration. Whenever it happened, whatever the reasons, one thing is certain—we are all the richer for it!

   Before the art of Wycinanki emerged, it had been the custom in Poland to decorate both inside and outside walls of buildings with

From the collection of Mr. and Mrs. Charles D. Curran

"Gwaizdy" or "Star" pattern from the Lowicz district in Poland. From the collection of Mr. and Mrs. Charles D. Curran

19

painted designs in bright colors. These paintings were usually decorative rather than representational in nature. Familiar themes, particularly flowers, trees and domestic animals, were used; but the renderings were often fantastical.

Furniture was another candidate for the artist's brush. The same intricate, elaborate approach to design so basic to the Polish artistic sense was drawn upon for cupboards, chair backs and chests.

It is from this background that the first Wycinanki emerged. At first, designs were cut from whatever paper came to hand—usually ordinary writing paper. They were of a single color and the subject matter was familiar—plants, animals and people. The earliest tool was one that almost all farm families had—the sheep shears. Skilled craftsmen could make surprisingly delicate designs with the tips of those long shears, which even today are the tools of choice among many Polish paper-cutters.

The cutting was (and is) done primarily by the women, perhaps as an ideal way to entertain children during long winter evenings. Quite naturally, seasonal decorations began to appear early in the history of Wycinanki.

Paper-cuttings were used at Christmas, of course, but Easter was the ideal time to make them, for the season came right after spring house-cleaning. The rafters had been dusted, and the walls, freshly white-washed, made a perfect background for the newly-cut Wycinanki. These were usually glued flat to the wall near its junction with the ceiling. The sides of the wooden ceiling beams became ideal locations for long horizontal arrangements. One wonders whether the Easter theme accounts for the lasting popularity of flowers, cocks and hens as subject matter for Wycinanki. And surely if we look back at the flower and bird motifs developed by the Chinese in celebration of *their* spring festival, we need no further reminder that the roots of culture are the same the world over.

As Wycinanki began to develop as a full-fledged folk art, certain distinct styles emerged.

The "gwiazdy" or "star" design was usually cut from a folded square of paper. Gwiazdy from the Kurpie district were made in single colors, and when opened had the appearance of fine lace doilies. The star cuttings from the Lowicz (pronounced *Wo-vitz*) district were more colorful, with bits of colored paper glued onto the basic cuttings.

Another style combined a star pattern with two cuttings done in vertical strips. These shapes were joined to form a riband with the star pattern at the top and two strips hanging from it—a creation similar to the show-prize ribbons we know in this country.

There was also a composition style called "kodry," done on a long horizontal axis. Many individual elements were glued on the wall in close proximity to one another to form a picture or scene. In the early days these kodry contained both decorative and representational parts. For instance, one popular theme was that of a village wedding. The realistic wedding party, in costume, might be surrounded by fantastical flowers and birds. Each colored shape was painstakingly cut from a separate piece of paper and glued into place. Over the years two distinct styles of kodry have developed. One features the decorative elements—usually imaginative, ornate flowers and birds in a long, balanced composition. The other portrays various kinds of work or ceremonies common to peasant life. The scene may take place either inside or outside the home, and it almost always features the colorful folk costumes of the area. As

The Kurpie district of Poland is well known for its wide variety of paper-cuttings featuring trees and fowl. From the collection of Mr. and Mrs. Charles D. Curran

A cutting by the author.

This family scene from Poland is notable for its fine detail—even the eyes and eyebrows are cut from paper!
Notice that the wall decorations are miniature Wycinanki. *Courtesy of Mr. and Mrs. Harold A. Beatty*

From the collection of Mr. and Mrs. Charles D. Curran

A riband cut by the author.

one may imagine, a tremendous amount of time and work is required for this style of paper-cutting. Unfortunately, it is rather rare nowadays.

Still another horizontal type of design was cut from a long strip of paper folded accordian-fashion. Simple shapes were cut out of the folded edges. When the paper was unfolded, it formed a decorative strip or border design. My husband's Polish grandmother always used this technique for homemade shelf-edging in her southern Illinois farmhouse pantry.

The most well-known modern styles of Wycinanki come from two districts. One is the kurpie cut-out. This is usually a symmetrical design cut from a single piece of colored paper, folded a single time, with spruce trees and birds as the most popular motifs. The second style comes from the area of Lowicz. It is distinguished by the many layers of brightly colored paper used in its composition. A Lowicz Wycinanki may feature a floral arrangement, or else a bright-feathered hen, or it may be a medallion which combines both themes. It almost always is composed of a black basic cutting with the colors assembled in layers on it. Although it is actually paper collage, from a distance it appears remarkably like a skillful painting.

Paper-cutting in Poland reached its zenith at the end of the nineteenth century, with many different regions expressing their individuality. Then, as the country became more urbanized, Wycinanki began to seem old-fashioned and provincial, and was given up by country folk in favor of more modern decorative forms. Ironically, it was the city people who saved the art from oblivion. Perceptive collectors began to see its value as a unique folk art. The Polish government became involved, sponsoring competitions and exhibits to encourage its continuance. Eventually many craftspeople began to work full-time to supply the demands of both foreign and domestic customers. New papers have been developed specifically for Wycinanki—particularly gummed-back papers. More precise technique, new and creative themes and larger dimensions are all helping to enrich the art.

The unique richness of paper-cut designs done in the Polish tradition is a special contribution to the artistic heritage of the world.

From the collection of Mr. and Mrs. Charles D. Curran

Silhouette portraits cut "at Richmond, Va., by Harriet Casper, December, 1787." From the collection of John A. Schapiro

Silhouettes

According to folklore, shadow pictures originated when a certain ancient lover returned home from a short absence to find that his lady had died. Rushing into the death chamber, he found a perfect likeness of her profile cast on the wall by the candle burning at the head of the bier. Reverently, he traced the likeness and preserved it, certain that it had been sent to comfort him in his grief.

Shadow pictures have existed at least since Etruscan times. Shadow figures of warriors and kings, lovers and families come down to us through the ages on vases and other artifacts left by several ancient civilizations. Shadow shows featuring figures cut out from heavy paper, leather and other materials, then manipulated against a translucent screen by means of sticks attached to them, are an ancient tradition in the Orient and Middle East.

Shadow portraiture has also been practiced down through the centuries in every conceivable medium. Profile portraits cut from paper can be traced back to 1699 when a Mrs. Pyburg cut the portraits of William and Mary of England. Many another famous personage, Goethe and Napoleon among them, speaks of having his "shade" cut.

Paper silhouettes reached their height of popularity in the eighteenth and early nineteenth centuries, literally foreshadowing photography. The materials were inexpensive and readily available, a skilled artist could capture a likeness in a matter of seconds, and several poses could be cut quickly, giving the sitter a choice if he wished one. Several copies

Male and female portrait busts dated 1812. The portraits were cut as negative shapes from light colored paper, then mounted on a dark background. Finally, the hair and other details were added by brushwork. From the collection of John A. Schapiro

24

This minister in his pulpit is an example of the sophistication brought to silhouette portraiture by August Edouart. From the collection of John A. Schapiro

could be cut at one time during the sitting, or copies might easily be made from the original at a later date. Any form could be recorded by means of shadow art—ships, pets, famous people, even events of importance. W. H. Brown (1808-1882), an American paper-cutter, made a six-foot-long cutting of the first excursion trip of the "DeWitt Clinton," the third locomotive built in America. The engine pulled a train of carriages, formerly horse-drawn, packed with important officials—all recorded by the skilled scissor-man. Brown also chronicled in cut paper the whole of John Calhoun's funeral cortège in 1850.

A few outstanding practitioners have raised shadow portraiture to the level of a fine art. Most notable was August Edouart (1789-1861), a Frenchman who entered the profession by chance when he had fallen upon desperate financial straits. It was Edouart who gave shadow portraits the name by which they are known today—silhouettes.

Etienne de Silhouette was the man elected Controleur-Général of France in 1757 through the powerful influence of Madame de Pompadour. Appalled by the extravagant spending practices of the Court and government of Louis XV, Silhouette took immediate steps to economize. He succeeded in cutting down on expenditures of the nobility, but his ambitious proposal for a new kind of banking system led to his downfall, after only eight months in office. Immediately the wags of the day began referring to anything that was inexpensive and common as a "silhouette." Edouart seized on the name as descriptive of his shadow portraits—inexpensive and available to anyone—and distinctive enough to set his work apart from much that was being produced at the time. Rejecting the host of patent inventions for casting and cutting shadows, he was a purist who cut only with the scissors, almost never embellishing his work with paint, pen, gilding or any of the other additions of his contemporaries.

Edouart worked first in England, Ireland and Scotland, then in France and finally in America. He made it his practice to visit the watering spots of the wealthy, such as Bath in England and Saratoga Springs in America. There he would set up a studio and advertise in the local papers. Many a sitter was so pleased with the results of Edouart's talent that he returned later with his entire family to be "cut." Business flourished.

A meticulous craftsman and bookkeeper, Edouart would cut two copies of each of his portraits—one for the sitter and one which he labeled with the sitter's name and title or rank, the date of the sitting, and other pertinent information. This copy was carefully mounted in a folio comprising a record of his work. In time, Edouart accumulated folios containing some 100,000 portraits. Most of these were full-length, owing to his conviction that head profiles alone could not give a true representation of character. Among his many notable subjects were five American presidents together with Sir Walter Scott, Henry Wadsworth Longfellow and Charles X of France, his entire family and their retainers.

In 1849, when Edouart was traveling to England from America, tragedy struck in the form of a shipwreck. Only a tenth or so of his folios survived. Edouart lived through the ordeal, but his health was undermined and his spirits utterly depressed by the loss of the record of his life's work. He never cut again.

Still, Edouart's influence lived on in the work of contemporaries and later silhouettists.

from Past to Present—and future

To the heritage of Hua Yang, Mon-kiri, Scherenschnitte and Wycinanki we can add many contributions from other nations: in England, the old-time music hall performers who developed paper-tearing into a fine art; the lovely paper hangings, church decorations and tablecloths made in Mexico; paper figures used for offerings and black magic in Mexico, Malaya and elsewhere; and silhouettes from all over Europe. Almost every culture has some history of paper-cutting.

Paper, scissors, a creative mind—history still can be made!

These ritual cut-out figures, meant to insure agricultural fertility, were made by the Indians of San Pablito, Puebla, Mexico. Courtesy of Fondo Editorial de la Plástica Mexicana

Embarking on the Craft

One of the most stimulating aspects of paper-cutting is its challenge as a totally creative medium, not only in results but in choice of working methods. To experiment with an untried technique is in itself a creative act; and any technique necessary to produce the desired result is a valid one to use. However, since some methods are well-tested and produce reliable results, they should be considered as the foundation on which to build your own inventive techniques.

For instance, most people feel more comfortable if they can sketch their designs before they begin cutting. This is a good practice so long as the sketch does not become a tight drawing. Remember that the scissors produce some curves and lines more easily than others, and if you try to force them to follow a sketch too precisely, you may be disappointed with the result. Further, if you tie yourself down to cutting out a finished drawing, you lose much of the fun of creative paper-cutting, and you risk ending up with a piece of work lacking the fresh, crisp quality that is such an appealing aspect of this art form.

I have been asked about using such drawing aids as a compass or ruler in the sketching stage of the work. I have no objection to this practice so long as it is not overdone. Sometimes, using a compass is the only way to get a good clean circular shape. But the design inside that circle should rely on the scissors to give it its final form.

Actually, I encourage a mixture of working techniques. By all means do some work with sketches. Use a compass and ruler when necessary. But at least part of the time, just "wing it" with the scissors.

As with the materials, subject matter for paper cut-outs is all around us—the trick is to become aware of it. Try to see what has become so familiar that it isn't seen anymore. Simple shapes such as those in a patterned rug, a swatch of wallpaper, a piece of furniture, or a wrought-iron fence can become the basis of a beautiful design.

There is a multitude of forms that we look at but don't truly see, either because we are so used to them or because subconsciously we have made up our minds that they hold no interest. For example, different styles of automobiles mean nothing at all to me; cars are just objects going by. But I noticed one recently because it had for a hood ornament a magnificently feathered cock. I tried to take a mental photograph of that bird so that I could adapt it to a paper-cutting. Since then I have noticed other car ornaments—a winged lady here, a bulldog there—and now I begin to perceive a whole new avenue of creative expression.

Try to see between and beyond the objects which fight to monopolize our attention. The negative spaces between clustered tree branches

in winter, or between the pickets of a fence, may make an interesting repetitive pattern suitable for duplicating with scissors. Decorative architectural details that we pass every day may hold an inspiration for a cutting design. Art work done by someone else, if particularly eye-appealing, can spark a design that will evolve into something totally new and personal.

Learn to look carefully, attempting to analyze just what it is that makes one shape different from another. Why does a clump of oat plants look different from a clump of wheat? What little curve of line will make a jack rabbit distinguishable from a domesticated one? What differentiates one roof or bell tower on the skyline from another? Why does a wild strawberry plant look different from a cultivated variety? What distinguishes the leaves of thyme from those of sage? Developing this kind of skill in observation can help an artist in any discipline.

And remember that contrast is the basis of appealing design. Sharp points together with blunt curves. Large with small. Fat with thin. Negative space with positive space. Long with short. Straight with wavy. Busy with plain. If you can get a good mix of these in your cutting, chances are that you will have an attractive finished piece of work.

In reading the descriptions of flat-paper and folded-paper techniques later in the book you may find that you want to start trying your hand as you read. And why not? There is no better way to learn paper-cut design. And since each of these sections contains material to stimulate both the beginner and the more experienced craftsperson, you may find yourself daring to attempt more advanced work sooner than you had hoped.

What to use and Where to find it

We are surrounded by materials suitable to the practice of paper-cutting. That unusual paper placemat at the restaurant can be brought home and recycled for use as part of a design. Thank-you notes, greeting cards, and even advertisements received in the mail may be scanned for an interesting style or color. Those mimeographed sheets the children keep bringing home from school are crisp, suitable in weight and usually plain-backed. Even paper towels have a pleasant texture, as does left-over wallpaper. File folders are a perfect weight for stencils. Let your "found" resources dictate your first work. After all, any paper that comes to hand can be used for practice; my first designs were cut from paper salvaged from a wastebasket.

As you become more involved in the craft and begin looking for suitable papers to buy, you will be pleasantly surprised at the wide variety of interesting papers that are readily available. In general, look for a light, crisp paper of rather fine texture. For most cutting, the weight should be somewhere between that of tissue and construction paper. If the paper is colored on one side and white on the other, so much the better, since this facilitates sketching.

Papers

Paper suitable for cutting is all around us, waiting for a moment of inspiration. We dropped this bundle of papers on to a lovely Chinese rug for photographing; and then realized that even those oriental butterflies can give ideas for experimentation in cut-paper.

Origami paper: Designed for use in the Japanese art of paper-folding, this paper comes in many colors. It is white on one side, crisp and lightweight—a good all-around paper for cutting. Its only drawback is that some of the colors may fade from prolonged exposure to light. Packets of origami paper are often available at Japanese import shops as well as craft and artists' supply stores.

Oriental tea-chest paper: This metallic paper was originally produced to line boxes used for storing tea leaves; its silver or gold coating helped seal out moisture. It is lightweight, white on one side, lovely to work with, and is available at some artists' supply shops and Oriental importers.

Gift wrapping: While gift wrap is heavier than origami paper, it may still be used for making designs with several repeats. It is as close as your drugstore, dimestore, or gift shop, and the variety of beautiful finishes—shiny or dull, patterned or plain—may give you some design ideas.

Silhouette paper: This black-coated paper was produced to meet the needs of the silhouette portrait artist. It has a nice dull black finish on one side and is white on the other. It is good for flat cutting, or for two- or four-repeat designs, but rather heavy for cutting through more than four thicknesses with comfort and accuracy. Always fold the black finish to the inside because it easily picks up oil from the fingers. Look for silhouette paper at artists' supply shops.

Coloraid paper: This paper is about the same weight as silhouette paper and is available in over two hundred colors, shades and tints. It is good for cutting flat or two-repeat designs or for cutting mirror-image shapes to be applied on top of a basic cutting. Fold it carefully; the colored coating has been known to crack along a fold. Most professional artists' suppliers carry it.

Gummed-back craft paper: Usually available in packages of assorted colors, this type of paper is marketed by several gift-wrap and craft-paper manufacturers. It is a bit heavy for multiple repeat designs but good for single or double-fold patterns, as well as for flat cutting. The lick-and-stick back makes it ideal for designs to be used on note cards which must be slipped into envelopes.

Rice paper: What we call "rice paper" is really made out of mulberry fibers. It is white and comes in several weights. A light, thin rice paper is good for Chinese-style flat-cut designs and can be colored with watercolors. The knife used for cutting should be kept very sharp in order to cut the fibers rather than tear them. Rice paper is available at good artists' supply stores.

Special papers: Special papers are sometimes available at import stores. A Polish import shop may carry Wycinanki papers, and colored Scherenschnitte paper may be found where German imports are featured. If you have friends or connections abroad, why not write and ask them to send a few examples of local papers to you?

Miscellaneous papers: Often paper manufacturers or supply houses will let you have "unusable" scraps free, or will sell you remnants at low cost. To win their good will, it is important to regard this as the courtesy that it is and not to browse or overstay your welcome.

Cutting Tools

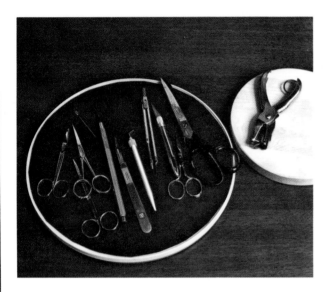

Left to right: sewing scissors, opthalmologist's scissors, dissecting scissors, straight pin, graphic pencil, surgeon's scalpel, frisket knife, compass, X-acto knife, embroidery scissors, sewing scissors—all lying on plastic turntable covered with black cardboard, paper punch resting on wooden cutting board.

Tools for paper-cutting are also easily accessible. Obviously, scissors are the most readily available, and, at least initially, you can let the scissors at hand dictate the kind of designs you cut. They may range from tiny curved cuticle scissors to giant tailor's shears. You can't expect to do large, sweeping curves successfully with tiny scissors, nor can you expect to make tiny intricate cuts with great big scissors, unless you are one of those Poles highly experienced with sheep shears! The best procedure is to experiment with what you have and then decide if you want to invest in a larger or a smaller pair.

My own favorite pair of scissors has blades about one and one-quarter inches long and handles about three and one-quarter inches long. This ratio makes for a strong, firm cutting capability. Also, the blades are beveled down to a fine point so that they do not leave a little tear in the paper at the end of the cut.

Scissors of all kinds are available at any good cutlery shop. Other sources to check are dressmakers' supplies, surgical supply houses, and art shops.

For those interested in trying knife-cutting techniques, I suggest looking into a number of possibilities.

There are many brands of craft knives on the market. Most of them have replaceable blades packaged in safety containers much the way razor blades are packaged. The X-acto Company offers many styles of punches and gouges as well as knives. All can be found at hobby, art-supply and craft shops.

Stencil knives and frisket knives are another possibility. Most come with disposable blades. A scalpel with a packet of replaceable blades, available at a surgical supply house, is inexpensive and super-sharp.

The Flat...

Paper-cuttings made with the paper laid flat on a cutting surface are usually cut with a knife. Designs cut in this fashion are not symmetrical as are those cut from folded paper.

In addition to the cutting tool (or tools if you are using punches or gouges also), you will need some kind of cutting base. A piece of cardboard, an old magazine or a wooden cutting board will do. You should have a needle and thread handy if you are going to fasten several layers of paper together to be cut at one time. And tape (transparent or masking) is needed to fasten the paper to the cutting surface.

I like to put the cutting board on a plastic turntable. This allows me to turn the work as I cut, thus keeping my arm in a comfortable cutting position.

Have on hand a pencil and a straight pin (for adding texture) in addition to a selection of papers.

...and the Folded

Fold-and-cut designs are produced in the same way in every culture. That is, the paper is simply folded two or more times. Then it is cut with knife or scissors. The difference lies in the choice of paper and in the treatment of the subject matter. The Japanese, for instance, favor simple geometric shapes or simplified forms from nature. The Polish, on the

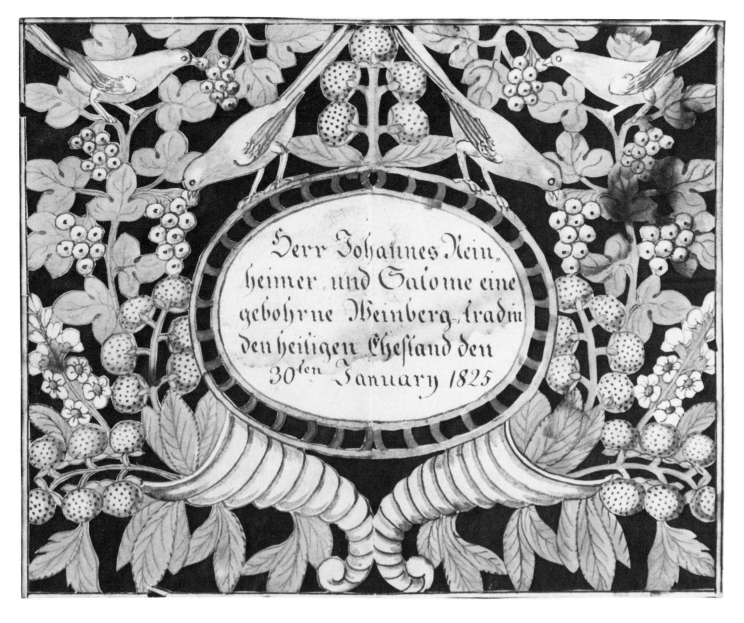

other hand, prefer intricately flowing lines filling every available space. They love fringed and decorated edges. Even when their subject matter is drawn from nature, they enjoy embellishing the natural shapes with additional decorations.

A word about terminology is important as we begin discussing fold-and-cut designs. Whatever design is cut into a *folded* paper packet, I call the *repeat*. When a paper is folded once, and a design is cut through both halves at the same time, the resulting art work will consist of two identical repeats.

When the paper is folded twice before cutting, it makes a packet of four layers to be cut at once. That design, therefore, will consist of four identical repeats when it is unfolded. We can go on until we produce designs consisting of sixty-four repeats.

It is important to select a light-weight paper for multiple-repeat designs, since you will be cutting through many layers at once. Origami paper is good for up to sixteen or even thirty-two repeats. A sixty-four repeat pattern usually calls for tissue paper.

The paper can be of any size and any shape. However, I usually start with a square. I recommend that my students do also, at least until they gain some experience.

A square can be folded in half down the middle to create a rectangular shape. However, I usually bring the diagonal corners together so that I have a triangular shape after my first fold. More shapes seem to fit naturally into a triangle. And it forms a base from which to go on to more complicated folding.

The secret of cutting from folded paper is this: *always preserve part of the folded edge.* Remember to leave at least part of every folded edge intact. If you do, you will never start with a lovely design in mind and end with a lap full of confetti. You may cut into a folded edge and take chunks out of it. You may even remove most of it. But you must not totally destroy it if you expect to have a design in a single piece when you finish.

Here are three other things to remember. First, a single slash made by the scissors will not show in the finished piece. The two edges will simply lay together and the cut will seem to disappear. Some amount of paper—whether it be a small sliver or a large chunk—must be removed in order for a cut-out shape to be seen in the finished design. Second, always cut into points and corners from two directions. This will give you a nice clean point or corner with no folded or ragged edges. And finally, as much as possible, keep your cutting hand stationary and turn the paper with your other hand as you cut.

Trying Your Hand

Designs Cut from Flat Paper

SUPPLIES:

PAPER (white or colors, rice, silhouette)
KNIFE
SCISSORS
PENCIL
CUTTING SURFACE (wooden board, cardboard, old magazine)
TURNTABLE (optional)
TAPE
NEEDLE AND THREAD (optional)
STRAIGHT PIN (optional)

PROCEDURES:

The Chinese tradition

1. Choose a finely grained paper. A coarse grain will tend to tear rather than cut when a knife is used.

2. Place the paper on the cutting surface—board, cardboard, or old magazine—and tape it in place. If you are cutting several copies at once, tack the stack of papers together around the edges with needle and thread. Then tape the sewn packet to the cutting surface.

3. Make your sketch on the paper, or on the top layer of the stack if you are cutting several copies. You can also use an existing cut-out as a pattern, in which case the cut-out can be fastened onto the paper with transparent tape. Stretch the tape right across the design to be sure that it is held securely. Then cut right through the tape as you make the cutting.

4. Using your knife, cut the smallest details first, then work to the larger ones. You may want to pick up the work and cut the final outline with scissors. A plastic turntable is an aid to comfortable cutting.

The German tradition

1. Use a single sheet of paper about the weight of typewriter bond or even heavier—a sheet from an artist's sketch pad is good. Silhouette paper is also good if you want a black shadow effect. Lay it with the black side down so that you can make your sketch on the white side.

2. You may follow the knife-cutting procedure above or do the cutting with scissors.

3. When the cutting is finished, add texture to the design by pin-pricking or slashing with the point of the knife.

fold-and-cut techniques

SUPPLIES : (for all multiple-repeat designs)
PAPER (origami, gift wrap, other light varieties)
SCISSORS
PENCIL
MOUNTING BOARD (poster board)
WHITE GLUE

PROCEDURES :

Two Repeats

1. Choose a square piece of paper of any size.

2. Fold it in half once. If it is colored on one side and white on the other, always fold it with the color to the inside.

3. Sketch half a design or begin cutting freehand with scissors. If the paper is thin, you can add stability by folding two or three sheets together and cutting several copies at once. Watch out for that folded edge! Remember, part of it can be removed, but some of it must remain intact. Use paper clips to hold some sections while you are working on others.

4. After the design is cut, unfold and inspect it. If you are dissatisfied with the work, refold it in either the same or a different way and do more cutting.

6. Open the design and press it flat under a magazine overnight. Or put it between two sheets of paper and press with a warm, dry iron before mounting.

7. See the section on "Mounting and Framing" for help in mounting your cutting.

Basically a two-repeat design, this scene featuring Adam and Eve was mostly cut out with the paper folded once. Then it was opened and each figure was cut individually.

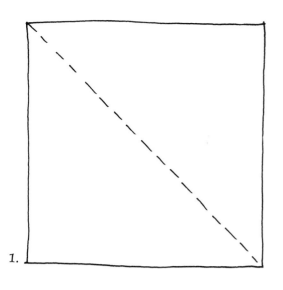

1.

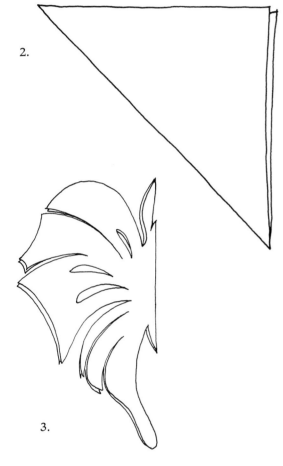

2.

3.

4.

Courtesy of Mr. and Mrs. Charles D. Curran

Four Repeats

1. Select a square of paper.

2. Fold it once, from one corner to the corner diagonally opposite, colored side in, to form a triangle.

3. Fold it again at right angles to the first fold. This will give you a smaller triangular packet consisting of four layers of paper. Notice that two sides of the triangle consist of folded edges; be careful of them.

4. Sketch your design or cut freehand. Be sure that you cut through all four layers at once. The more interesting you can make your cuts at this stage, the more intricate the design will appear when it is unfolded.

5. Open one fold at a time, very carefully. Press out each fold between your thumb and forefinger before going on to the next one. Check to see if the design pleases you. If not, refold the paper in the same or a different way and continue cutting.

6. Place the completed design under a heavy book or magazine, or press it between two sheets of paper with a warm, dry iron.

7. See the section on "Mounting and Framing" for help in preparing the work for display.

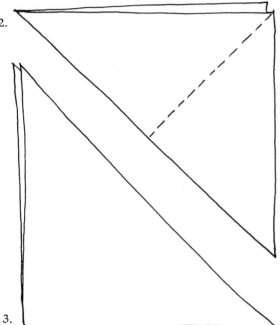

Another design produced by following the first three steps and varying step 4.

38

Six Repeats

1.

2.

3.

4.

5.

Eight Repeats

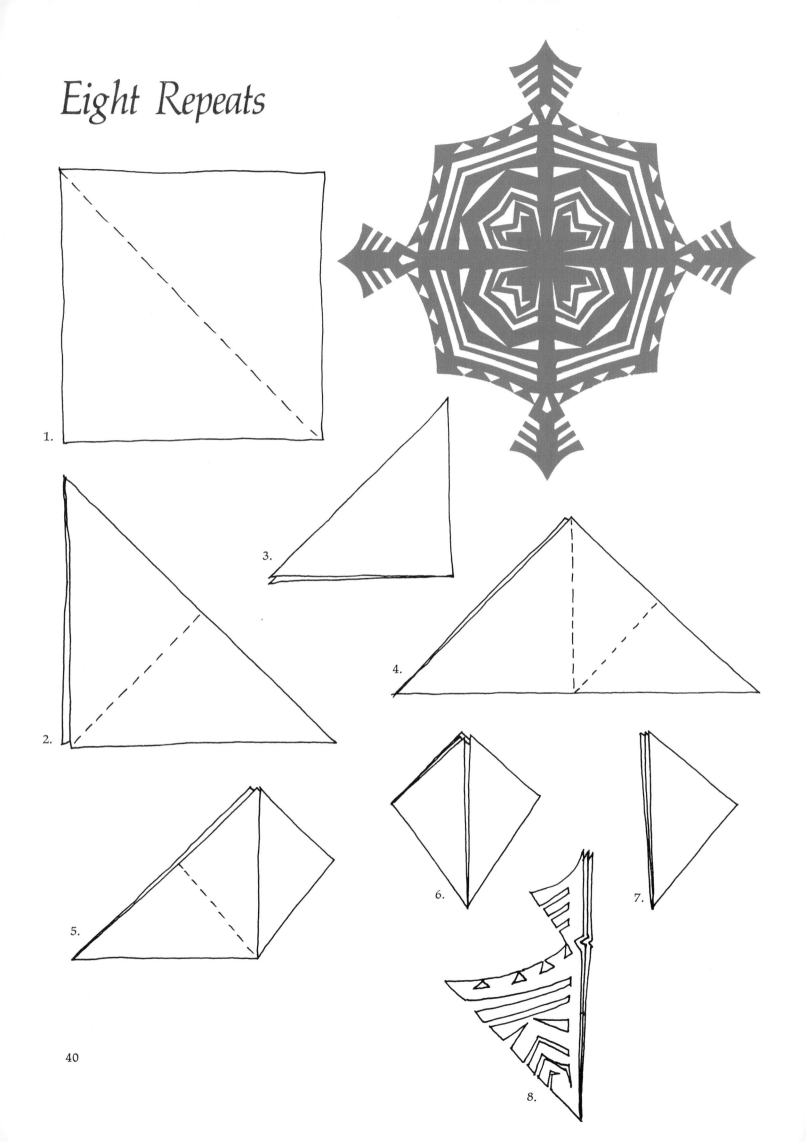

1.

2.

3.

4.

5.

6.

7.

8.

Ten Repeats

1.

2.

3.

1/3

2/3

4.

5.

6.

7.

As a little girl I heard the old story of how George Washington went to Betsy Ross with a sketch for a flag which included six-pointed stars. Her response, as it came down in history, was: "A fine design on the whole, General, but those six points will have to go! Why, with just a few folds and a single snip of the scissors, I can make you five-pointed stars with ease." I credit that sentence with driving more craft people crazy than any other statement in history.

Perseverance does prevail, however, and anyone can learn to fold and cut a five-pointed star from paper. I learned, and turned them out. But it was never easy, until Freddie Hanson came into my life. I have known Freddie since the age of five. (He's now nine.) He came to Cub Scout den meeting one night and announced that he and his grandmother had been visited by Betsy Ross's great, great, great granddaughter, who had shown him how to cut a five-pointed star. He proceeded to take a scrap of paper, fold it and cut the star. Without one bead of sweat. I could hardly hide my chagrin.

Trying to appear suave, I encouraged him to "show the other boys," so that I could secretly study his technique. Before long, we were up to our knees in five-pointed stars.

So what I offer as the ten-repeat pattern is Betsy Ross's five-pointed star, à la Freddie Hanson. But don't stop at the star alone. Turn it into a handsome ten-repeat paper-cutting!

Twelve Repeats

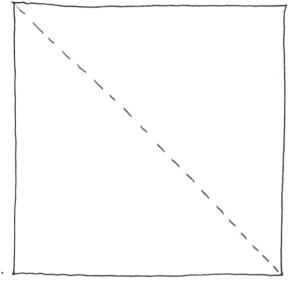

1.

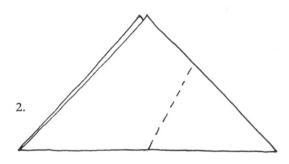

2.

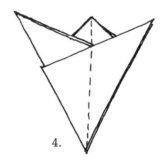

4.

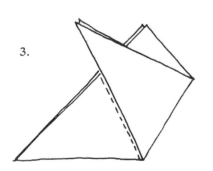

3.

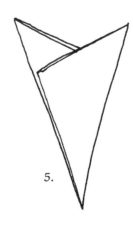

5.

6.

Sixteen Repeats

1.

2.

3.

4.

5.

6.

7.

8.

9.

Thirty-two Repeats

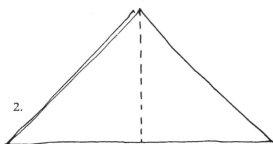

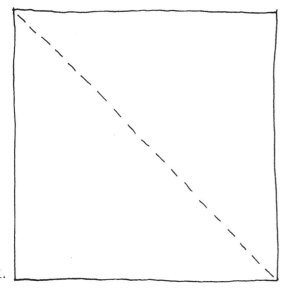

Sixteen layers of origami paper are about the maximum number that most scissors will cut with any degree of comfort and accuracy. So to make a thirty-two-repeat design you may want to switch to tissue paper. Or you can cut the pattern in two stages as indicated in the diagram.

The tricky thing to remember is that you have three sets of folded edges to watch out for—the two outside edges and the set of folds down the center.

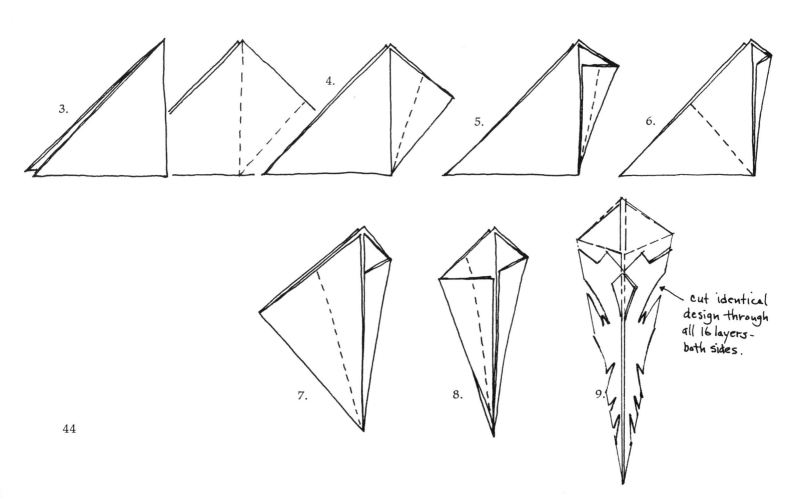

cut identical design through all 16 layers- both sides.

Sixty-four Repeats

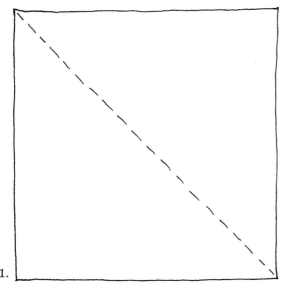

1.

2.

At last we come to those elegant, doily-effect cut-outs from the Kurpie district in Poland. I have succeeded in producing this many repeats only by working with tissue paper. Perhaps someone else will have better luck than I have with a slightly heavier paper.

A good pair of scissors should be able to handle the thirty-two layers of tissue paper used in this style of cutting. Again, guard the three sets of folded edges.

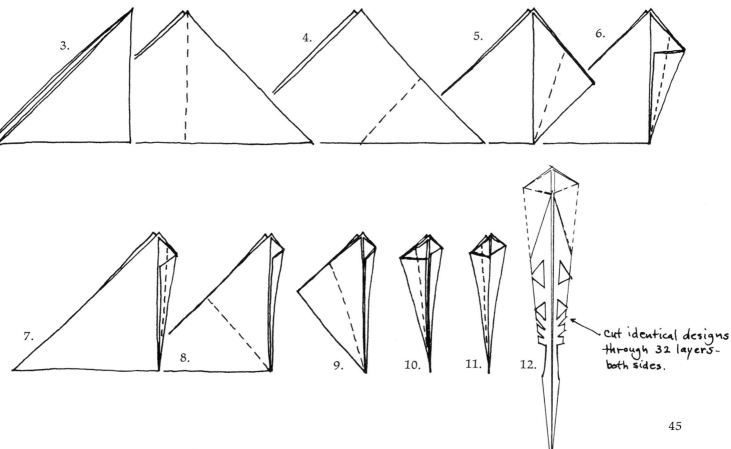

3.

4.

5.

6.

7.

8.

9.

10.

11.

12.

cut identical designs through 32 layers—both sides.

Border Designs

1. Cut a strip of paper to about eleven inches by four inches. Other sizes can be used, but this is a good size with which to practice.

2. Fold it according to the diagram. Note that the important folded edges are parallel. Designs can be cut along each folded edge and also along the ends of the folded packet. Just be sure that some part of each folded edge remains intact.

3. Unfold and press the design before mounting it. The Polish people often use this type of cutting to make the grass and borders for their cut-paper scenes.

Paper Dolls

Paper dolls can be produced from the same kind of folded packet.

1. Fold a strip of paper as you did to make a border design.

2. Sketch half of a figure—a person, animal, plant, or whatever you fancy—or cut it freehand. Be sure that the center of the body is positioned at the edge of the packet composed of two folded edges. If you are making dolls, their arms should extend to the side which includes the loose edges. For a droll effect, you may want to cut the eyes with a paper punch.

3. Unfold the paper and consider whether you might enjoy some further decoration. If so, embellish each figure with hand drawing (eyes, whiskers and the like), or cut shapes from other colored papers and glue them in place on each figure. Or bring the loose hands of the two end-figures together and fasten them with tape or glue. Now you have a circle of figures that will stand alone.

Breaking Down the Design to Find the Repeat

Somewhere you may see a design worth using as a model for your own fold-and-cut work. Analyzing such a design to find the repeat is the key to duplicating it; but the analysis may be puzzling, especially if the design is printed and there are no fold lines showing.

Here is a method that should unlock the most unyielding design secret:

1. Select a strip of paper with a straight edge and lay it on the design so that the edge passes through the center point and divides the design in half. You will find that it begins to look simpler already.

2. Now take a second strip of paper and lay it at right angles to the first one, so that the straight edge also passes through the center point of the design. Now you have isolated one-quarter of the design. Does that quarter look as though it is the simplest element in the whole, or does it look as though it might be divided to get a simpler repeat?

3. Use a third strip of paper to divide the quarter section in half. Now you have isolated one-eighth of the design. Is that the simplest element?

4. If not, use a fourth strip of paper to divide this one-eighth section in half. Have you isolated the basic repeat? In our illustration we have. But it is possible to continue dividing sections in this manner until even smaller repeats are isolated.

5. Once you have isolated the simplest section of which the whole is composed, you have the basic repeat. Now keep that repeat marked, and count how many times it is appears around the entire design. When you have that number, simply refer to the Table of Contents for instructions on folding your paper to produce the same number of repeats. Use the isolated design section as a model either for a sketch or for freehand cutting.

Reproducing Classic Ethnic Designs

The techniques explained in the previous chapter are basic to paper-cutting: they constitute the fundamentals of the art form. Once you are comfortable with them, you can put them to use in creating more elaborate designs in one or several of the ethnic traditions previously discussed. We shall take a close look at three of these traditions: the Chinese, Pennsylvania German, and Polish. In each case the designs involve multiple colors, providing a new avenue of creative expression for the paper-cutter.

The Chinese Tradition

So you are intrigued with the brightly colored Chinese paper cuttings? Perhaps you would like to reproduce one, either as an experiment with the technique, or because you have just the spot on the wall to display it.

We have noted that the Chinese dye stacks of paper-cuttings in brilliant colors, all in a single operation. Most of us do not have access to the dyes to do an authentic job of coloring in this manner. However, with a little thought as to subject matter and style of drawing, and with a set of watercolors and a sheet of rice paper, a reasonable facsimile can be produced.

To get some ideas about subject matter, you might study the Chinese cuttings reproduced in this book, or in books on Oriental art forms available at the library. You will notice a heavy reliance on nature and natural objects and on characters and scenes from mythology for subject matter. The composition is very flat: figures and objects do not diminish in size as they appear further away from the eye of the viewer, as they would if drawn in normal perspective. Instead, things in the foreground are placed near the bottom of the composition, and those in the middle or background are put higher up in the picture.

Often, the Chinese paper-cutter will enclose his composition in a geometric form—a rectangle, octagon or square, for example.

SUPPLIES:
PAPER (rice paper, sheet from artist's sketch pad)
KNIFE
PENCIL
TAPE (transparent or masking)
PLASTIC TURNTABLE (optional)
WATERCOLOR SET (a simple children's box will do)
BRUSHES
CONTAINER OF WATER
CLEAN CLOTH
CUTTING SURFACE (wooden cutting board, cardboard, old magazine)

PROCEDURE:

1. Select a piece of white paper.

2. Make a sketch if necessary.

3. Fasten the paper to the cutting surface with tape at the edges. If you have a plastic turntable, place the paper (and cutting surface) on it.

4. Cut out the design with a knife, starting with the smallest details and working up to the larger shapes. Refer back to "Designs Cut from Flat Paper" for help if necessary.

5. Once the cutting is completed, lay the design on a clean piece of paper.

6. Use watercolors to paint the design. Use clear, vivid colors and do not let them flow together too much. Keep the hues clear and bright by rinsing the brush thoroughly before switching to each new color.

7. Let the design dry completely while it is still lying on the clean paper. If it should stick to the paper and become difficult to remove, slip the craft-knife blade under it to loosen it. If it is crinkled from the watercolor, press it with a warm, dry iron after placing it between two layers of paper. Then it will be ready to mount.

The Pennsylvania German Tradition

Courtesy of Hallmark Cards Incorporated

People interested in antiques may find themselves esepecially drawn to the Pennsylvania German style of paper-cutting. The charm of the style lies in its seeming artlessness and child-like quality. For example, figures are drawn using stock forms, with all details shown in dark lines, hats perched directly on tops of heads, and colors laid on flat with little or no shading. Scale is often determined by the size of the space being covered rather than by reality—a vase of flowers may be drawn as large or larger than the human figures. Birds may be as massive as trees or houses. And everything is presented with a liberal amount of imaginative decoration —the birds may have flowing striped feathers where no real bird ever grew such a feather; flowers may have some polka-dotted petals and some plain ones; deer may have branches of foliage sprouting from their heads. Artwork in the Pennsylvania German style was a means of having fun—and we can have fun with it too.

I suggest using opaque watercolors or acrylic paint for coloring these cuttings. Many of the paints used in American folk art were opaque in appearance. When choosing colors, remember that the old pigments came from natural sources such as clays, brick dust, berries, or the soot from lamps, so that they were rather subdued in appearance.

In order to re-create the somewhat primitive charm of this art form, your colors should not be too obviously planned. Folk artists didn't worry much about whether this color went with that one: they used whatever colors they thought were pretty, from whatever they had on hand.

Another way to make a multi-colored Pennsylvania Dutch design is to cut all of the elements from different colored papers and then arrange them in a composition on a mounting board. We shall explore this technique more fully in a later chapter.

SUPPLIES:
PAPER (typing bond, drawing paper)
SCISSORS
KNIFE (optional)
STRAIGHT PIN (optional)
OPAQUE WATERCOLORS
BRUSH
WATER
CLEAN CLOTH

PROCEDURE:

1. Select paper suitable to the type of design you have in mind. If it is going to be a flat-cut design, the paper can be heavier than that used for a fold-and-cut design.

2. Cut your design according to the instructions for flat-cut work (page 35) or for any of the fold-and-cut techniques (pages 36-46).

3. If you have used a fold-and-cut design, press it open under a magazine or warm iron to smooth the folds.

4. Embellish some areas of the design with pin-pricks or slashes of the knife point if you wish.

5. Lay the work on a fresh paper and apply colors. Keep the colors bright and clear by rinsing the brush thoroughly before switching to each new color. If you wish, mute the colors by mixing a tiny amount of black into each one as you use it.

6. Let the art work dry completely before attempting to mount it.

The Polish craftspeople are probably the most masterful at creating many-colored works of art using cut paper alone. Their fascination with intricate design has led them to produce paper-cut pictures in which even buttons and buttonholes are cut from paper and glued in place.

Aside from the elaborate and painstaking detail in Polish Wycinanki, its most distinctive characteristic is the liberal use of black as a foil for brilliant colors. Again, in keeping with folk art, the color arrangements are seldom planned in advance; rather they are allowed to happen as the work progresses.

In the first chapter we introduced some of the many styles of paper-cutting in Poland. We can look at them in greater detail now. Let's begin with a relatively simple floral arrangement similar to those produced in the Lowicz region of Poland—an area well known for using bright colors in costumes as well as in art work.

The Polish Tradition

(A)

(B)

(C)

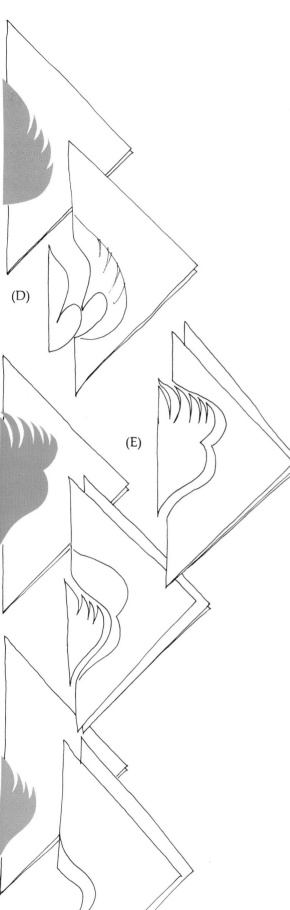

(D)

(E)

SUPPLIES (for all Wycinanki designs):
COLORED PAPERS (origami, gummed-back craft paper, gift wrap or specialized papers from Europe)
SCISSORS
PENCIL
MOUNTING BOARD
WHITE GLUE
TRANSPARENT TRACING PAPER
TAPE (transparent or masking)

PROCEDURE:

1. Select the colored papers you wish to use in your design—as few as two or as many as seven or eight. The ground is usually cut first. In our illustration, green paper is the choice for the base.

(A) 2. Fold the paper in half once.

3. Sketch or cut freehand the foliage and flower stems.

4. When the cutting is completed, unfold it carefully, pressing it open with the thumb and forefinger. Lay this piece aside and go on to develop the blossoms.

(B) 5. Select the colored papers you wish to use for the large center flower of the arrangement. I usually use the darkest color for the base cutting, and work up through the layers until the lightest color is on top.

6. Fold the paper for the basic flower shape once.

7. Either freehand or from a sketch, cut the basic blossom shape. See the diagram.

8. Plan each shape to be placed on top of the basic blossom so that it is successively smaller, in order that all of the colors may show.

9. Select your second color and fold it in half.

(C) 10. Place your base flower, folded in half, on top of the folded paper selected for your second color.

11. Outline the flower in pencil lightly. This will set your limit for cutting the second flower shape—it must be smaller than the first.

12. Cut a smaller shape within the sketch you have made of the base flower.

(D) 13. Select your third colored paper.

14. Using the second colored shape as a pattern, trace it onto the third color, just as you did the first time.

15. Cut the third shape so that it will be smaller than the second.

16. Continue with as many colors as you like, making sure that each is smaller than the one before.

(E) 17. To create two identical flowers, one for each side of the arrangement, use the same basic procedure but fold two sheets of each color together and cut them at the same time to produce two sets of identical colored shapes.

18. Once all of the shapes are cut, you can begin assembling them into a design on the mounting board.

Once you learn the basic technique, you can go on to create floral arrangements as elaborate as you wish—up to and including the long horizontal kodry so popular among the Polish peasantry.

(A)

The Lowicz Birds

Lowicz-style birds are created in a manner similar to the flowers. However, they are not cut on the fold. The bird (rooster, peacock, dove or whatever) is first sketched, then cut out with scissors, and then decorated with different colors built up in layers just as are the flowers described above. The basic bird shape is usually cut from black with the colors applied on top. Usually the bird stands on a branch or foliage base.

PROCEDURE :

1. Select the color for your basic bird shape.

(A) 2. Cut the basic bird freehand, or from a sketch. You may want to sketch the bird you see illustrated here, or use a pattern derived from a book or magazine, or perhaps create your own. When I am executing Lowicz-style birds, I usually put three or four sheets of paper together and cut out several at once. It saves time, and it's fun to see in how many different ways the same shape can be decorated.

3. Select the colored papers for the head, wing and tail decorations.

(B) 4. Place the bird-cutting on one of these papers and sketch around it lightly. This will indicate the shape you must work within when making the head, wing and tail decorations.

(C) 5. Cut the basic wing and tail shapes. They will then become the patterns for the next color you select.

Again, each colored shape should be made successively smaller until you have cut as many layers as you wish for your design.

(D) 6. Cut the branch or greenery for the footing, using flat or folded paper.

7. Assemble the whole, using the section on "Mounting and Framing" as a guide.

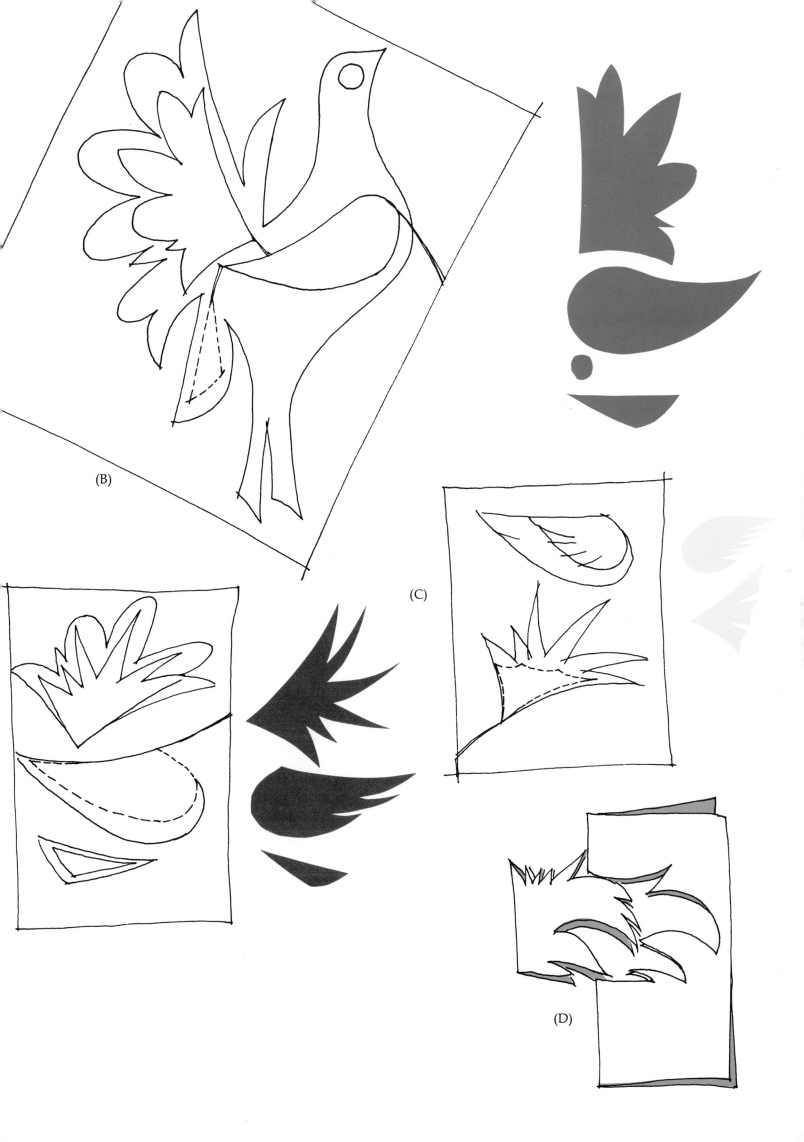

(B)

(C)

(D)

(A) (B) (C)

The Kodry

As we have mentioned, the kodry style of paper-cutting usually features some type of work or ceremony common to the Polish peasant folk. It almost always includes figures in colorful peasant costumes. It usually contains some background details—either wall decorations for an interior or grass and sky representations for an exterior scene. Usually, a combination of flat-cut and fold-and-cut techniques is used. All cutting is done with scissors.

Although traditional ethnic pieces are shown in our illustrations to clarify the working method, contemporary scenes are also a fertile field for the imagination. Why not sketch one, and try it?

PROCEDURE:

(A) 1. Make a sketch or trace a scene in enough detail so that the basic shapes are all clearly indicated. A traditional female figure clearly shows the head, blouse, skirt, arms and legs. A man's figure is made up of head, jacket, trousers and boots. Background material should be sketched in its proper relationship with the rest of the scene.

2. Place a sheet of transparent tracing paper over the entire sketch and trace every shape to be cut from one color, starting with the color you plan to emphasize. If black is your choice, for example, you might want to trace the man's hat, coat and pants, and the woman's skirt, vest, boots and hair.

(B) 3. Tape the piece of tracing paper with its outlined shapes to a piece of black paper, and cut out all of the shapes. Cut right through both the tracing and the colored paper. You will notice that some of the shapes touch each other and seem to form a single larger shape. You may cut them out as a single large shape; however, it may become necessary to snip them apart to get a good fit during the mounting procedure.

4. Place the shapes on the mounting board in the approximate position they will occupy in the finished work. Do not glue them down at this time.

57

(D)

(E)

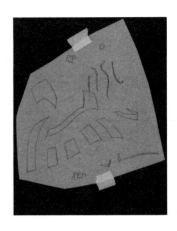

(F)

(C) 5. Using a fresh sheet of transparent paper, trace all the shapes of the next color.

6. Tape this sheet to the new color and cut out all of the shapes.

7. Place them in their relative positions on the mounting board.

8. Repeat the process for each of the colors in the picture. You may want to use some of the fold-and-cut methods discussed earlier to create trees, flowers, grass or other forms for the background.

(D) 9. Once all of your pieces are cut, glue them to the mounting board in their proper positions. Use only a small bit of glue on each piece. If you are using a gummed-back paper, moisten it only slightly. You may have to trim some shapes to make them fit properly.

Now it is time to add the detail that makes these kodra so rich-looking.

10. Place a piece of transparent tracing paper over the scene glued to the mounting board.

(E) 11. Sketch onto the tracing paper any detail which will make the scene more interesting. It might be a series of stripes on the skirt and trousers, a band of embroidered flowers on the sleeves of the woman's blouse, a sash, or clouds in the sky.

(F) 12. Now put another sheet of tracing paper over this sketch and follow the same procedure as before:

—trace all of the shapes to be cut from one color;

—tape the tracing to paper of the proper color and cut out all the shapes;

—lay them on the finished picture, trimming some with scissors if necessary to get a pleasing fit;

—repeat the process for each color.

(G) 13. Once all the details are cut and laid in, glue them down carefully.

Using this method, an artist can be as detailed as he or she likes—right down to earrings and shoelaces.

(G)

The Lowicz Medallion

The medallion is distinguished from the "star" pattern in that it usually features only two repeats, while the star may have from four to sixty-four repeats. The basic cutting is usually executed in black, but any color may be used.

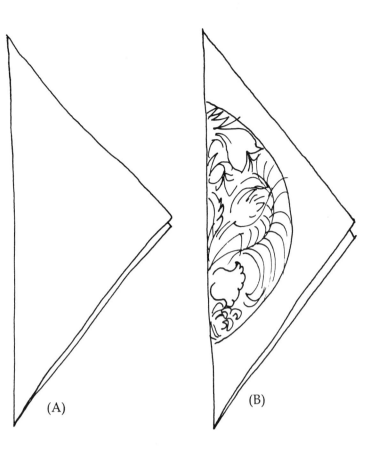

(A)

(B)

(C)

PROCEDURE:

1. Select a square of black paper of any size for the basic cutting.

(A)   2. Fold it in half once.

(B)   3. Cut freehand or sketch a design. You may want the aid of a compass to get a good half-circle shape. Flowers or birds or both are the most popular motifs for this style of cutting.

(C)   4. Cut out the design. Beware of the folded edge—do not totally destroy it. If it is necessary to puncture the paper with the point of the scissors to cut out a particular shape, puncture at the middle of the shape and work to its edge.

(D)   5. When the cutting is complete, unfold the design carefully and press it flat.

6. Select the colored papers for the decorative elements on top of the basic cutting. You will need two pieces of each color.

7. You will want to cut mirror-images of each of the decorative shapes— one for the right and one for the left of the basic cutting. This is accomplished by placing two sheets of paper face-to-face and cutting through both at the same time.

(E)   8. Using parts of the basic cutting as patterns, pencil around the necessary shapes onto the colored paper. This will tell you the shapes within which you must work when cutting the decorative elements to be layered on top of the basic cutting. Remember that each color becomes the pattern for the next smaller layer.

9. Once all of the designs are cut, glue the basic black cutting to the mounting board. Consult the mounting section for guidance in getting the cutting mounted straight.

10. Add the colored decorative shapes on top of the basic cutting in the proper position and sequence to complete the design.

(E)

(D)

61

The Riband

The riband is an old style of paper-cut decoration not seen much any more. At one time, each region in Poland had its own style of riband. Some of the styles have been duplicated in materials more substantial than paper for use with wedding flower bouquets. Each riband consists of a circular medallion at the top with two or more streamers hanging from it. I am including them here because they are lovely to look at, great fun to make, and can easily be adapted for use as "blue ribbon" awards.

PROCEDURE:

1. To make the medallion, select a square of colored paper and fold it as though you are making a sixteen-repeat design (page 43). Trim away the loose edges with a curved cut, then cut a decorative edge along the curve.

2. Unfold the paper and you have a circular shape with a decorated edge. This is the base upon which you will build a decorative design. It may be a series of fold-and-cut designs layered atop one another from large to small as you see in the illustration. It may be a floral arrangement such as that shown on page 52; it may be a Lowicz-style medallion, or anything else that can be cut from paper. Let your imagination take over.

3. Once the medallion is finished, lay it aside and select the paper for the streamers. You will need two strips to make two streamers.

4. Fold it according to the instructions for making border designs (page 46).

5. Cut a decorative design along each end.

6. Unfold each streamer.

7. From other colored papers, cut designs and mount them on each streamer. Again, let your imagination go and see what you can come up with. The two streamer decorations may be identical or different.

8. Finish the bottom of each streamer with additional border designs cut from colored paper.

9. Glue the streamers so that they hang from the back of the medallion, scissors-fashion.

10. Use the finished riband "as is" for a prize ribbon or glue the whole to a mounting board for display.

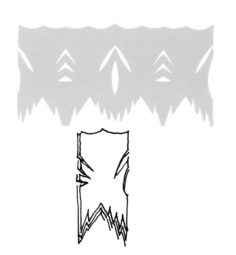

Mounting and Framing

Wall display

Adam and Eve shown off on a blue background with a wide white mat. A thin blue line drawn about one-quarter inch around the mat opening helps carry the color. A cutting by the author.

Obviously, a finished paper-cutting can be a delicate thing indeed, and it requires careful handling. For this and other reasons I recommend pressing the cuttings, at least overnight, before trying to mount them. They can be placed between the pages of a magazine, under a book, or under a sheet of plexiglas—the better to reflect on them while doing other things. If you are in a hurry, put the cutting between two pieces of paper and press it with a warm, dry iron. This must be done with great care because the cutting will tear easily even with the paper protection. Pressing gets those folds under control so that the piece will lie flat on the mounting board.

Paper-cuttings can be mounted onto a number of different surfaces for wall display. A stiff piece of paper might be adequate for some. I steer away from construction paper because the colors tend to fade quickly under continued exposure to light. Poster board from the dime-store is a good general-purpose mounting surface. It is fairly rigid and comes in many colors. If the particular color you want in a board is not available, mount your work on a piece of colored paper, and mount that in turn to poster board. Cutting the mounting board to a standard frame size will make it easier to frame the work. These sizes (all in inches) are: five by seven, eight by ten, nine by twelve, eleven by fourteen, and sixteen by twenty.

A fancier background for mounting can be made by laminating a piece of fabric such as gingham or calico to a stiff cardboard. This is done by placing a piece of fusible web (available at fabric stores or departments) between the board and the fabric, then ironing the fabric with a steam iron. When it is cool and dry, mount the paper-cutting on it with white glue. There are several brands of fusible web on the market—all suitable.

There is a useful procedure for getting the work to stick to the mounting board.

1. Start by making a light pencil line down the center of the board as a guide.

2. Turn the cutting face down on a clean surface and put a few tiny spots of white glue along the center axis of the design. Even if the design is intricately cut, there should be room for some minute dots of glue.

3. Now carefully lift the work, turn it over, and align the center axis with the pencil line on the mounting board—it is easy to see through the cut-out spaces in the design.

4. Cover it with a clean paper and gently press down the glued area. Now the center of the design is anchored to the board.

5. Gently lift the right-hand side of the design, lap it over to the left, and apply a few tiny spots of glue to it here and there.

6. Roll that side back to its correct position and cover it with a clean paper.

7. Working from the center of the design to the edges, carefully press it down. If you keep pressing from the center out, you should be

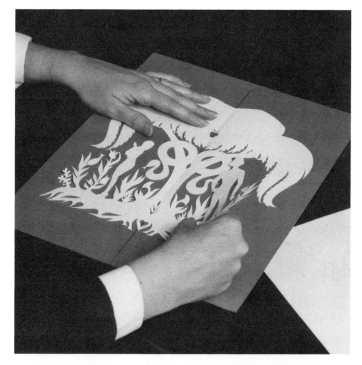 

 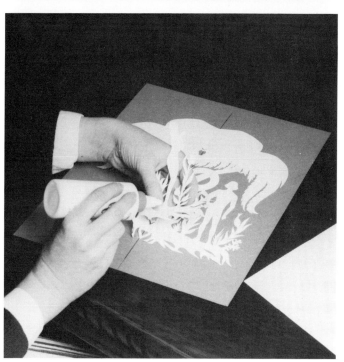

successful in eliminating any wrinkles. When the design is totally smoothed down, remove the clean paper.

8. Now lap the left side to the right and follow the same procedure to glue that side of the design. Protecting it with a clean paper during the pressing-down process not only keeps it clean but avoids a possible tear in the design if it is rubbed too vigorously.

When gummed-back paper is used to make the cutting, follow this procedure: Place the design face down on a clean surface and moisten it with water. Turn it face up and align it with the guideline on the mounting board. Cover it with a clean, dry paper—a paper towel is good—and press gently, working from the center out to the edges, until it adheres.

This process has to be accomplished quite quickly, because the paper may tend to curl after the water has been on it a few seconds.

If you are adding layers of colored paper, work with these next. Start with the largest shapes first, then work up layer by layer to the smallest. Always use tiny spots of glue only, and cover the cuttings with a clean paper before pressing them down.

There are many brands of white glue on the market, most of which are suitable. I like an applicator top that allows you to control the amount of glue flowing from the container. Some of the glues dry more quickly than others. When first applied, most glues will show on the front of the design as a bubble or wrinkle. But such flaws will disappear as the glue dries.

Although I have tried many techniques for sticking paper-cuttings to mounting boards—rubber cement, sprays, dry mounting, laminating, hot and cold techniques—I keep coming back to the spots of white glue. Most work is cut from such light-weight papers that it cannot stand up to a coat of adhesive. I suspect that work cut from the heavier papers such as silhouette paper or Coloraid might take a spray adhesive satisfactorily. But lighter papers are too fragile for this treatment. Of course, as new glue products come on the market they can be tried, but experiment with a piece of work about which you don't have strong feelings!

Once you have succeeded in mounting your work, think about matting and framing it. In choosing a color for the mat I encourage my students to relate it to one of the colors in the art work. Color tones in the room or setting surrounding the paper-cutting should also be taken into consideration.

Mats can be bought ready-made at craft shops, art supply houses, and framing stores. They are made either from smooth or pebble-surfaced cardboard, and are available in a wide selection of colors. Some of the more expensive ones are covered with fabric. If you prefer, you can cut your own mat from whatever you have on hand. Be forewarned, however, that making a neat job of a homemade mat is not easy.

Framing is the final step. Paper-cutting is such a delicate art form that care must be taken lest the frame overpower the work itself. For any paper-cutting on which you have lavished a great deal of care and skill, consultation with a professional framer might be a good idea.

If you buy one of the many types of ready-made frames, I would suggest that you look for a simple, thin frame with a lightweight appearance. I personally prefer wood to metal. Wood frames can be painted easily in order to coordinate them with the art displayed within.

Once the work is framed, a piece of brown paper should be glued to the back so that it covers the entire back side of the piece. This helps to keep out dust and moisture. Insert two eye hooks and a wire for hanging, and your work of art is ready to admire and enjoy!

Window decorations at Christmas or any time of year. White tissue-paper designs preserved in clear plastic folders share the panes with smaller designs laminated between layers of waxed paper (center, left).

It is possible to mount paper-cuttings so that they are visible from both sides. To achieve this unusual effect, use a transparent plastic report cover such as those available at dimestores and office suppliers. Simply insert the cutting between the folder's two clear plastic leaves; the friction of the plastic will hold it in place. Hang the folder with the fold to the bottom, using a needle to string a loop of thread through the top edge. The report cover can be cut to any suitable size.

I particularly like to see star patterns, cut from white tissue paper, mounted in this fashion. They have a lacy, delicate, frosted-glass appearance when hung where sunlight from a window can shine through them.

Another interesting technique consists of laminating the paper-cuttings between two pieces of waxed paper. Although not permanent, this method is easy, fun, and results in an interesting window decoration.

Lay a piece of waxed paper on the ironing board. Arrange one or more paper-cuttings on it. Cover them with a second piece of waxed paper. Press gently with a warm, dry iron. Don't overdo it. You want the wax in the middle to melt and form a bond; you don't want to burn it away. After pressing, allow the paper to cool, then trim the edges with scissors.

This is an exciting way to cover a viewless window. Use double-faced transparent tape to fasten the paper to the windowpane.

Back and Front Display

Cards and notes of endless variety can be made with cut-paper designs. The first and third from the top come from Poland, and are reproduced through the courtesy of Marie Piechocka Edmonston. The second is also from Poland. The fourth from the top comes from China. And the bottom one is my own design.

How You Can Use Paper-Cuttings

Note Cards

The art of paper-cutting lends itself beautifully to use as a means of communication. Anyone who can remember laboring over an ornate, hand-crafted Valentine for a youthful sweetheart knows that the work carries a message more eloquent than any words which may accompany it.

Johann Uhlman with his cut-paper love letter, and scores of Pennsylvania Dutch with their elaborate cards and Valentines, used the art form to convey greetings and sentiments. The Polish craftspeople still use paper-cuttings as primary forms of decoration on their note cards for all seasons. In my own collection is a lovely card from China which features a scene viewed through a cut-out, hand-painted window. Handmade note cards make any message seem especially thoughtful.

All you need is a fairly stiff piece of paper, folded in half. Simply cut your design in the proper size and glue it on what will become the front of the folded card. I like to use gummed-back craft paper for this kind of project because it can be pressed absolutely flat, enabling you to slip the finished card into the envelope without danger of catching and tearing the design.

If you don't have suitable paper on hand for making the folded card, it is possible to buy card blanks at art supply stores and some stationers. Choose cards made of stiff paper with an interesting texture, either in white or an appropriate color. Matching envelopes are usually provided.

Valentines are a highly creative art form. They can be entirely hand-cut, or your own cutting can be combined with store-bought decorations such as doilies, ribbons and prints. If you accomplish a really fancy design, remember to mark the envelope "Please hand cancel" before you mail it, so that your creation is less likely to be damaged during its trip through the mails.

Paper-cut Frames

How often have you come across some pointed saying or poetic quotation which has caused you to wish that it could be framed and hung on the wall? And yet, chances are that if you *have* framed it, nobody has noticed it. It's dull-looking.

The solution is paper-cutting! Give that motto a facelift. Make it noticeable by surrounding it with a cut-paper frame. Many of the styles of cutting discussed earlier in the book can be adapted to this use.

A favorite photograph can often be enhanced with a mat decorated with paper-cutting in keeping with the mood of the picture.

Take that wedding invitation, surround it with a paper-cut mat, put it in a frame and give it to the bride.

All it takes is paper, scissors, and a liberal amount of imagination.

This photograph was taken the day of my paternal grandparents' wedding. Decorating the mat with cut-paper flowers was, for me, pure delight.

Christmas Decorations

Christmas—what a marvelous season for those of us who must make things if we are to feel truly fulfilled.

Paper cut-out Christmas cards can range from a simple snowflake on a blue background to an elaborate nativity scene done in the Polish kodra style. I like to use simple, stylized forms of familiar subjects— candles, greenery, Santa Claus and the like. These can be pasted down either on cards made at home out of stiff paper, or on commercially made card blanks. Again I recommend gummed craft paper for the cutting because of its "lick and stick" feature.

Polish Christmas Card. Courtesy of Mr. and Mrs. Harold A. Beatty.

Shadow cards

Here's a technique sure to appeal to children—and to anyone else who's never outgrown a love for splattering paint around.

Cut a design from a medium-weight paper; ordinary writing paper will do. Fold a half-sheet of construction paper once to form the card. Lay the construction paper card in the bottom of a cigar box from which the top has been removed. Now place the paper-cut design on what will be the front of the card and secure it with a couple of straight pins pushed down through the design, through the card and into the bottom of the box. Place a ruler across the top of the cigar box so that it makes a bridge.

Now load an old toothbrush with paint. Don't overdo it—you may want to blot the bristles on a rag. Tempera or any water-base paint will do. Hold the ruler securely with one hand, and with the other push the toothbrush down toward the bottom of the cigar box at an angle, against the edge of the ruler. The paint should spatter onto the card in the bottom of the box. Continue to spatter-paint the card all over by moving the ruler about. With a little practice you will learn to place the paint anywhere you wish.

After you have covered the card with as much or as little paint as you want, remove the ruler and allow the card a few minutes to dry partially. When the paint is about half-dry, lift the card out carefully and remove the pins and the paper-cutting from it. You may want to use a pair of tweezers. If you wait until the paint is completely dry, the cutting

may stick to the card. Once the paper-cutting is removed, its shadow remains—floating in a colored mist! Now let the card dry thoroughly.

If you want to use the paper-cutting for making another card right away, blot it dry on both sides with an old rag and go to it again. After you have made all the shadow cards you wish, let the paper-cutting dry completely and then glue it to a card for still another effect.

Tree and Window Decorations

Endless Christmas tree decorations can be made using paper-cutting techniques. Fold-and-cut designs from about three to five inches in diameter make unusual and inexpensive ornaments. Protect them in cut-down, clear plastic report covers, as mentioned earlier, before they are hung on the tree.

Other decorations can be created by cutting simple shapes—for example, an angel, bird, trumpet or wreath—from stiff paper or poster board. Each base cutting is then decorated on both sides with more intricate designs cut from colored paper, and the finished work is pierced with needle and thread to make a hanger.

Garlands for the tree can be made from paper which is folded accordian-style and then cut into an interesting seasonal design. Garlands can be glued end-to-end indefinitely to produce a chain that will encircle even the fullest Christmas tree.

Christmas tree decorations made with paper-cutting techniques lend a bright warmth to a wintery branch. The top three are cut from black poster board with designs from colored paper added. The fourth is a fold-and-cut design encased in a plastic folder. And the bottom is a "stained glass" design cut from two layers of black paper with colored tissue paper sandwiched between.

A Polish tree-trimming tradition consists of cutting miniature Wycinanki designs from colored paper and gluing them to blown-out egg shells. (For directions on blowing out eggs, see page 92). The resulting ornaments can be hung on the tree by stringing a ribbon through the holes in the eggshell.

"Stained glass" is fun to make. Using a craft knife, cut a design through two pieces of medium-to-stiff paper. Black is a good color choice. After the design is cut, put one of the two sheets aside, and glue bits of colored tissue paper over the openings in the design of the other. Cover the tissue-paper side with the second copy and glue the two together so that the tissue paper is sandwiched between them. Hang the completed work with a loop of thread. "Stained glass" cuttings can be made in any size—small enough to hang on the tree or large enough to cover a window or door.

And what Christmas would be complete without a liberal sprinkling of white "snowflakes" cut from paper and scattered on windows, walls and tree, and hanging from the chandeliers?

Needlework

Paper-cutting techniques are highly useful in accomplishing various forms of needlework. As we have seen, one of the earliest uses of paper-cut designs in China was as a means of creating embroidery patterns. Cutting embroidery patterns from paper is a common practice in Mexico today.

In the interest of exploring this technique, I consulted Elizabeth L. Kidder, President of the Baltimore chapter of the Embroiderers' Guild of America, Inc. She too had read of this technique, but never having practiced it, she embarked on a project utilizing a cutting I had made with a knife in the Chinese manner. Beth Kidder proceeded to turn my design into a piece of needlework of startling beauty.

As we soon found, the creative possibilities of this technique are exceptionally interesting. The needleworker uses the paper-cut design as a canvas and the floss as paint. No two designs need ever come out the same, even if they start with the same paper-cutting. We wondered, too, about the possibility of doing the original cutting from Pellon instead of from paper, using scissors. This would add body to the finished embroidery work.

Embroidery courtesy of Elizabeth L. Kidder

Embroidery Over Paper Cut-out

For the following section, the author and publisher are indebted to Elizabeth L. Kidder.

Embroidery courtesy of Elizabeth L. Kidder, from a design by the author

For the background fabric, any medium- to heavy-weight dress material will do, as long as it is firmly woven. Broadcloth, sailcloth and denim are all good choices. Very light fabrics may be puckered by the embroidery; very heavy fabrics may be difficult to embroider. Knit fabrics should be avoided unless they are bonded and not "stretchy"; loosely woven fabrics such as butcher linen may not hold the stitches firmly, yielding an uneven result.

As for the thread, cotton six-strand floss of number eight pearl cotton does beautifully; buttonhole silk, sold at many notions counters, is another possibility. Good quality cotton embroidery floss feels silky to the touch. Whatever thread you choose, only one strand at a time should be used in the needle. Otherwise you will find it nearly impossible to achieve a smooth effect.

In general, the proper-size needle for any given thread will be thick enough to prepare a hole in the fabric large enough for the thread to slide easily. If the thread keeps falling out of the eye of the needle, you will know that your needle is too large. For the single strand of cotton floss in the design illustrated, I used a "between" (a short needle with a round eye) in a fairly small size. A number six crewel embroidery needle is about right for the number eight pearl cotton thread.

The paper from which you cut your design should match approximately the colors of the thread you intend to use for the embroidery; white for pale colors, dark for darker colors.

PROCEDURE:

1. Mount your cloth in an embroidery hoop and stretch it tightly.

2. Put a little Sobo or other good glue on a scrap of paper.

3. Using a toothpick or fine brush, put a little glue on the back of each section of the paper cut-out. Place the cut-out on the stretched fabric and press it lightly in place. On the flower design shown, a spot of glue was applied near the tip and near the center of each petal and leaf. The tip of the stem and the center of the flower were also glued; most of the stem was too slender to glue easily.

4. Let the glue dry several hours.

The usual way of starting embroidery thread is to take a few tiny back stitches in the center of an area that later will be covered with embroidery. However, this is difficult to do through the glued paper, so start your first thread by knotting the end and leaving this knot on the *right* side of the fabric about three inches from where you plan to start stitching. When the thread is all used up in embroidering, finish off the end by running it through the back of the completed stitching for about one and one-half inches and cutting it off. Then cut off the knot, thread that end into the eye of the needle, and finish it off the same way. After the first thread, all threads can be started by

Chinese slippers—well worn, well loved. The embroidery work provides inspiration.

running them through the back of some completed stitching.

In our illustration, all or the embroidery is satin stitch, except for the center of the flower, which is made up of solid French knots. Satin stitch looks easy, but it takes some practice to make it smooth, with good clean edges. Satin stitch looks even smoother if done at quite a steep slant. To help achieve a good slant, make your first stitch near the center of the petal or leaf; work from the center out to the tip of the petal, then slide your thread through the back of the completed stitching to the center and complete the petal.

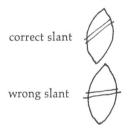

correct slant

wrong slant

Working satin stitch in a hoop, using only one strand of thread at a time, practicing the stitch until you develop a rhythm, working on a slant, and working over a paper cut-out are all techniques that will help you make smooth satin stitch with a clean, even edge. The cloth should be framed so tightly that you cannot put the needle in on one side of the shape you are embroidering and out on the other in one motion.

For this particular example, I worked the large flower petals in two shades of yellow cotton floss, using them in alternate petals; it may look as though more shades were used, because of the play of light on the shiny cotton floss

satin stitches. The three tiny flower petals were done in ombre (shaded) cotton floss; about every eighteen inches, the color of the floss changes gradually from pale yellow to brown. I decided to have each petal shade from light at the center of the flower to dark at its outer tip, and therefore I cut for each tiny petal a strand of floss with one end pale yellow and the other end brown. I threaded this into the needle, knotted the pale end of the strand, and started stitching at the end of the petal nearest the flower center. When using the shaded cotton, don't start at the center of the petal as you would when working with unshaded thread, or the shading will "break" at the center of the petal. If you run out of thread before finishing the petal, take care that the beginning of the new thread matches the end of the old one.

All three leaves were worked in number eight pearl cotton; one of them was done in shaded pearl cotton. The stem is in cotton floss.

When all of the satin stitching is finished, fill the center of the flower with French knots, for a change of texture. Use a single strand of pearl cotton, or four strands of floss. To give an interesting color, I used two strands each of two different pinks threaded together into the needle.

The technique of embroidering over paper gives a good clean edge to the stitching and offers an easy outline to follow. It is especially useful in embroidering on dark-colored or other hard-to-mark fabric. In cutting paper patterns for this sort of embroidery, remember that satin stitches longer than about one-half inch are apt to loosen and shift. In conclusion, this method renders especially striking those works made for display, where laundering is not a consideration.

Applique

A natural extension of fold-and-cut paper techniques is their application to fabric. Paper-cutting is an ideal way to originate designs for appliqué work. Many old album-quilt block designs were worked up from fold-and-cut paper patterns. "Hawaiian" quilts are made from a series of blocks appliqued with a fold-and-cut design. Sometimes one large fold-and-cut design covers an entire quilt or coverlet.

Clothing decorations, wall hangings and all kinds of accessories for the home can be done in applique. A good excercise for the beginner, and a conversation piece, is an appliqued sofa pillow:

An applique quilt, 1840-1870. Courtesy of the Maryland Historical Society, Baltimore

SUPPLIES:

THREE SQUARES OF FABRIC 17″ x 17″—all in coordinated colors
PAPER 15 inches square (shelf paper, gift wrap, brown paper)
TWO SQUARES OF UNBLEACHED MUSLIN—17″ x 17″
PILLOW STUFFING (shredded foam, dacron fluff)
SCISSORS
PENCIL
STRAIGHT PINS
NEEDLES
THREAD

PROCEDURE:

1. Fold the paper according to any of the following techniques discussed earlier in the book. I recommend sticking to the simpler folds (two or four repeats) at first.

2. Sketch a design. At the risk of seeming overcautious, I suggest that it be fairly simple since it must be stitched all the way around by hand. There is no reward in placing too many tedious details between you and the enjoyment of the finished design!

(A) 3. Once the design is sketched, go back and add a line about one-eighth inch around the entire form and around every interior section that is to be cut out. The reason for this is that all cut edges must be turned under during the applique process.

4. Cut out your paper design.

(B) 5. Unfold it and place it on one of the fabric squares to see if it pleases you. Remember that the finished work will be a little thinner than the pattern because all cut edges will be turned under.

6. Select the square of colored fabric from which you wish to cut the design.

7. Fold it just as you folded the paper before. You may want to press it lightly to flatten it a bit.

(C) 8. Now, with the scissors, cut *one* repeat from the paper pattern. To do this, simply cut down any two adjacent folds in the paper pattern from the outer edge to the center of the cutting. This repeat now becomes the pattern for cutting the fabric.

(D) 9. Place this pattern on the folded fabric, according to the diagram, and pin it securely with straight pins.

10. Cut around the pattern with good sharp scissors.

(E) 11. Remove the pattern and unfold the fabric design.

12. Center the fabric design on the fabric square you have chosen to be the face of the pillow, and pin it in place.

13. Baste about one-quarter inch in from the edge, around the entire perimeter of the design and around all interior cut-outs. Also run a basting stitch down the center of any large areas on the design to help hold them in place while you are working.

14. Beginning at any point on the design, fold under the cut edge and sew it to the backing, using a blind or overcasting stitch. Proceed around the entire outer edge and around all interior cut-outs. Remove basting.

15. Once the design is entirely stitched, place the block with the appliqued design face down on the third square of fabric. Secure it with pins.

16. Sew a half-inch seam around three sides. Leave the fourth side open.

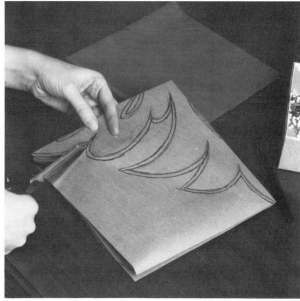

(A)

(B)

(C)

17. Turn the fabric so that the seams are to the inside. Work the corners out to a sharp point. Do not poke them with the scissors—work them with your fingers.

MAKING THE PILLOW FORM:

1. Lay the two squares of unbleached muslin one on top of the other and stitch half-inch seams around three sides.

2. Turn the resulting form so that the seams are to the inside.

3. Fill the form to a comfortable thickness with shredded foam or dacron fiberfill.

4. Turn in the raw edges of the fourth side and sew by hand or machine stitching. Your pillow form is now complete.

Insert the pillow form into the appliquéd cover, turn in a half-inch seam along the fourth side and stitch invisibly by hand. The pillow is finished!

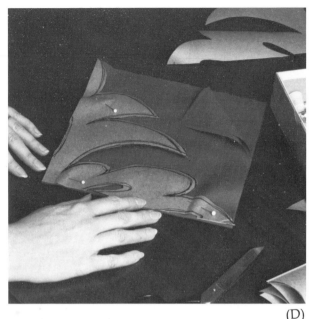

(D)

(E)

The pillow on the left is the one we have used for our illustrations. Perhaps seeing it together with the quilt and the two piecework pillows will inspire you with new design ideas. Quilt and applique courtesy of Marion Jablonski

Trapunto

Trapunto is an Italian word meaning "to embroider." It has come to refer to a particular style of needlework which involves stuffing two layers of fabric to produce a design in relief. Designs can be accomplished through the use of cut-paper patterns. Trapunto can be used on quilts, wall hangings and clothing accents. I suggest making a pillow to learn the technique.

SUPPLIES:

TWO SQUARES OF FABRIC (17″ × 17″—one for the front and one for the back of the pillow)

A SQUARE OF MUSLIN (17″ x 17″—it can be a piece from an old sheet or pillow case)

PAPER, 15″ SQUARE (shelf paper, gift wrap, brown paper)

SCISSORS

PENCIL

BALLPOINT PEN (optional)

STRAIGHT PINS

KNITTING NEEDLE

DACRON FLUFF

PROCEDURE:

1. Place the square of fabric that is to be the front of the pillow face down on a smooth surface.

2. Place the muslin square directly on top of it and pin the two together.

3. Now baste them together by hand or machine. Run the basting from corner to corner forming an "X," and from center edge to center edge forming a cross. The object is to fasten the two layers together firmly, so that they will not slip. When this is done, put the fabric aside temporarily.

(A) 4. Fold the square of paper, and cut a simple two- or four-repeat design.

(B) 5. Now cut the design apart into simple sections. For instance, if you should decide to cut a butterfly shape, it would first be cut as a two-repeat design with a fold down the middle. Then it would be snipped apart so that it is in three parts: two matching wings, and a symmetrical body. Or if you are making something like a flower, each petal can become a separate part.

6. Now lay the paper-cut pattern pieces on the muslin side of the two fabrics which have been basted together. Adjust the design so that it is in the proper location on the square, and so that the pieces are in the proper relationship to each other. The sections may be touching in such a way that only a single line separates them. Or they may be set slightly apart.

(C) 7. Once you are satisfied with the positioning, secure the design with straight pins.

(D) 8. Trace around each pattern piece with a pencil or ballpoint pen.

9. Remove the pins and pattern pieces.

10. By hand with small running stitches, or by machine, stitch around each piece of the design, following the pencil or pen lines carefully. Use a regular to small stitch length, according to the weight of the material.

Trapunto pillows add a touch of elegance. Courtesy of Mary H. Prince

(A)

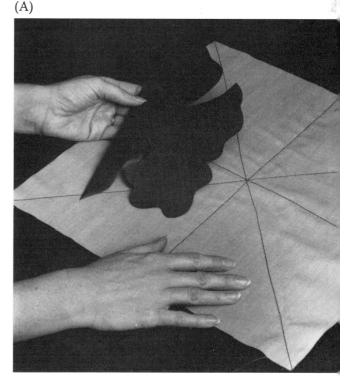

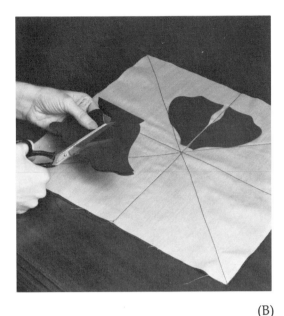

(B)

(C)

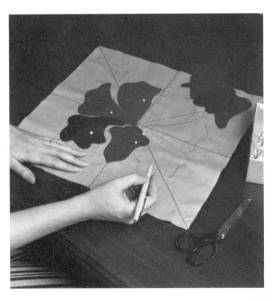

(D)

11. Once the shapes are outlined in stitching, snip and pull out any basting that falls within the borders of the design.

12. Now, with small sharp scissors, carefully cut a slit through the muslin *only* of one of the shapes composing part of the design. For example, if you are doing a butterfly in three sections, you may choose to stuff the body first. Carefully cut a slit *across* (not along the length of) the body section approximately in the middle. Start and end the slit no closer than one-eighth inch from the line of stitching that makes the outline of the shape. (E)

13. Stuff that section to the desired thickness with small bits of dacron fluff. If the space is too small to push the stuffing in with your fingers, use a blunt knitting needle to be sure that the fluff reaches all the way to the border of the design, and into all of the little nooks and crannies.

14. Once the stuffing is in place, whip-stitch the slit securely closed.

15. Now go to the next shape to be stuffed and repeat the process:
   —Cut a slit through the muslin *only*, beginning and ending no closer than one-eighth inch from the stitching lines. Make the slit even shorter if you can, but leave enough room to get the stuffing in.
   —Stuff the shape.
   —Close the slit by hand-stitching.
   —Proceed to the next shape.
   Once you have stuffed all the shapes composing the design and the slits are closed, you are ready to construct the pillow cover.

16. Lay face up, on a flat surface, the square of fabric forming the back of the pillow.

17. Lay the trapunto-work piece face down on top of it.

18. Pin the edges of three sides together evenly. Leave the fourth side open.

19. Sew a one-half inch seam around three sides.

20. Turn the resulting cover right side out. Work the corners out to a square with your fingers.

21. Follow the directions in the appliqué section for making a pillow form with unbleached muslin and shredded foam, or purchase a sixteen-inch by sixteen-inch pillow form.

22. Insert the pillow form into the cover.

23. Turn in a one-half inch seam on the fourth side and blind stitch it by hand.

24. Remove the basting remaining on the front of the pillow. You're finished!

(E)

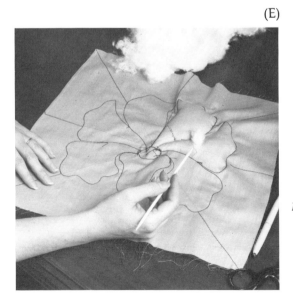

Design by Mary H. Prince

Decoupage

Decoupage can take many forms as these pieces by Carol Lynch Perry show. The gold and silver design in the background was applied behind glass. The scrollwork on the red and black box was cut freehand from metal-leafed paper then buried under many layers of varnish. All of the black on the gold and black box is paper. You can see similar patterns laying in front of the box, cut from paper and waiting to receive a special finish. The small leaf and scroll designs scattered about are all cut from paper that was first leafed with metal. Examples of the leafed paper occupy the lower left corner of the picture.

Decoupage is defined as "the assembling and composing of many related cut-outs into a composite whole."[1] It comes from the French word "couper" meaning "to cut," and has come to mean the art of decorating surfaces attractively and artistically with paper cut-outs. The surface may be wood, metal, ceramic, glass or papier-maché, with the paper cut-out first glued down and then covered with many coats of varnish. Or it may be cut-paper placed under glass, on silk, or on a mirror and not varnished at all.

Decoupage as we know it came about in Europe in the eighteenth century. At that time many original engravings were cut up and used to decorate furniture in an effort to imitate the Chinese and Japanese lacquer-work so much in fashion at that time. The art has been practiced in America for about fifty years.

Decoupage in its pure form still means choosing printed designs, cutting them out, perhaps coloring them with great care, and affixing them to some kind of surface. Actually, although at first it seems hard to believe, among the wealth of printed designs available, the really creative person often finds nothing truly expressive of himself. This, however, is why paper-cutting is so compatible with other crafts. For the beginner or for the experienced decoupeur looking for new directions in the craft, creating paper-cut designs can add an exciting and challenging dimension to decoupage.

Careful choice of paper for decoupage projects is important because you are creating a permanent piece of art work. Decoupage involves a good deal of work, and it would be most discouraging to find your efforts spoiled by lack of care in the first step of its production. For this reason, you will want to select a paper of good quality which won't fade or deteriorate. It should be reasonably thin so that it will blend well with the surface it is to decorate. Japanese tea-chest papers come in gold and silver, Coloraid papers can be bought in any and all colors, and book-binding paper and certain gift wraps are also good choices.

[1] *Manning on Decoupage*, by Hiram Manning, Hearthside Press, New York.

If you want to decorate your own paper, for a special effect, a bond paper with some rag content is a fine, strong paper to choose. It can be decorated in numerous ways. The design can be cut first, then colored by putting it on a piece of waxed paper and dabbing it with acrylic paint of a creamy consistency, then transferred to a clean sheet of waxed paper to dry. Or texture can be added by coating the cut-out design with artist's modeling paste brushed on with a soft bristle brush. If a single coat does not give enough texture, let it dry and apply a second coat. When the texture is satisfactory and the cutting is dry, color it with acrylic paint, metal leaf, or any of the gold brush-on products that are first mixed with water, then applied.

If you want to experiment with a really fancy finish, try metal leafing. Leaf the entire paper before cutting the design. This technique is done in stages. First, spray the paper with several coats of a good, heavy acrylic sealer. This does not mean drenching the paper—several light coats will do the job, but one or two heavy coats will not. Once the sealer is dry, spray it with a light coat of a good gold size. Lay on the silver leaf, pure gold leaf (or dutch metal, which is also gold in color but is composed of several alloys rather than pure gold). Let it dry, spray it with a fine mist of acrylic sealer and do your cut-out.

If you have used dutch metal or silver leaf, the paper can also be tarnished or antiqued for a special effect. A tarnishing solution can be made by mixing a pea-size amount of sodium sulfide crystal in two ounces of hot water. Dab it on the leafed paper with a piece of cotton and watch it change from a magenta color to a silvery blue-green to the last stage of burning, a rusty black. You can stop the burning at any time with a dry piece of cotton dabbed over the leafed surface.[2] Allow the paper to dry, seal it with a mist of spray sealer, and then create your own cut-out design.

To accomplish antiquing, dip a stiff-bristled tooth brush in a ready-mix antiquing solution and then flick it onto the leafed paper by running the index finger across the bristles. Allow it to dry, then spray it with a light coat of varnish. Cut your design when the varnish has dried.

The proper cutting technique is helpful in making cuttings for use in decoupage. In so far as possible, the cutting should be done with the cutting hand slightly tilted at the wrist so as to create a bevel on the edge of the paper as it is cut. This makes for a smoother transition between the paper design and the surface to which it is applied. If a knife is necessary, as for cutting tiny, lattice-like designs, use a surgeon's scalpel and hold it, too, at an angle so that instead of making a perpendicular cut, the cut is made on a slant through the thickness of the paper.

There is a national organization for people interested in decoupage as a fine art—The National Guild of Decoupeurs, Incorporated. One of its directors, Carol Lynch Perry, was quick to see the relationship between creative paper-cutting and decoupage and has kindly shared her knowledge and experience with us here. She points out that in keeping with its goal to support and perpetuate the fine art of decoupage, the Guild offers certificates of competency for its members to achieve, be they Laymember, Journeyman, or Mastercraftsman. A certificate in Creative Cutting is offered under the Mastercraftsman category—a goal the paper-cutting techniques set forth in this book may help one achieve.

[2] *The Art of the Painted Finish for Furniture and Decoration*, by Isabell O'Neal, William Morrow and Co., Inc., New York.

Stencils

Stenciled floors and stenciled floorcloths both date from the eighteenth century. This is an example of a contemporary floorcloth. Courtesy of Floorcloths, Inc., Annapolis, Maryland

Stenciling is an age-old technique for applying a design to any given surface. We have seen how ancient Japanese artisans used stencils in decorating fabrics and clothing, and we have talked about stencils used to embellish walls, floors, and furniture in early America. Now let's look at a technique for making stencils, using paper-cutting skills as a means of getting a clean, symmetrical stencil design.

SUPPLIES:

PAPER (typing bond, gift wrap, brown paper)

SCISSORS

PENCIL

WAXED STENCIL PAPER

CRAFT OR STENCIL KNIFE OR SURGEON'S SCALPEL

MASKING TAPE

STENCIL BRUSH

PAINT (see below)

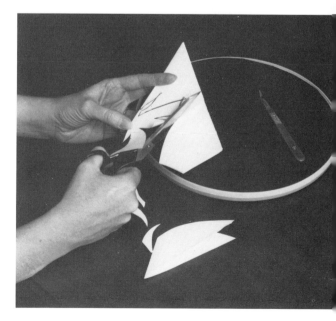

(A)

(B)

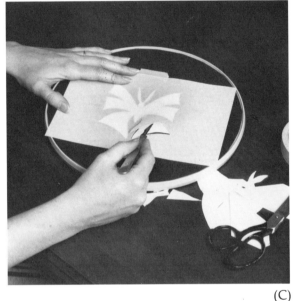

(C)

PROCEDURE:

1. Cut a design from plain paper using the flat-cutting technique or the two-repeat method. Keep it simple to begin with—make a single positive shape such as the butterfly you see pictured. I suggest avoiding negative shapes cut out of the design's interior at this stage. That sort of thing can come later as you gain experience in stencil cutting. (A)

2. Place your cutting on a fairly hard cutting surface—cardboard or a thick magazine will do. I like to put the cutting surface on top of a plastic turntable so that I can turn it for easier cutting. (B)

3. Place a piece of waxed stencil paper on top. You should be able to see the cutting through the stencil paper. If not, switch to a darker background under the cutting to provide more contrast.

4. Once the background is satisfactory, tape the waxed stencil paper in place over the cut-out design. (C)

5. Cut the stencil with a craft knife, stencil knife or surgeon's scalpel. Follow the outline of the paper pattern carefully. Turn the work so that your hand and arm are always in a comfortable cutting position.

Once the stencil is cut, it can be used in any number of ways: to apply designs to wooden plaques, boxes or furniture; to decorate fabric for towels, placemats and clothing; to adorn cards, mats and picture frames; and even to decorate walls and floors.

A NOTE ON PAINT:

It is important to use the right kind of paint for the stencil project you undertake. Various kinds of wood may take acrylics, oil paint or enamel, but fabrics require special paints developed for use on cloth. These can be made permanent by ironing the fabric several times on the reverse side after the stenciling is completed. The hotter the iron, the more permanently the paint will set. Since natural fibers such as cotton, wool, silk and linen can take the highest heat, they are the most satisfactory to work on. Man-made fibers and blends can be used, but since they cannot be ironed with as much heat, the colors remain fast only if these fabrics are given the mild laundry treatment their manufacturers prescribe.

For stencil designs on paper, any paint normally used on paper will do. The mixture should be rather thick and is best applied with a blunt stenciling brush in an up-and-down stippling motion, working from the outer edge to the center of the design.

As you gain experience you will want to experiment with more complicated designs. And try using several colors in a single design by cutting a separate stencil for each color.

The transformation of the once-drab van into a sleek mobile pleasure-house, complete with creature comforts inside, and a pictorial expression of its owner's personality outside, is a fascinating sidelight to twentieth-century culture. The interest in motor vans is a logical extension of the highway-oriented life-style of young Americans; often the custom features in these homes-away-from-home are completely made and installed by the proud owners. But what of the intricate symbols and elaborate murals that are so prominently displayed on many vans? Surely they too result from the same impulse toward individual expression and creativity which produced the lovely Window Flowers of China, the elaborate kodry of the Polish peasant folk, and the carefully wrought valentines of the Pennsylvania Dutch schoolboy. And although van-painting requires more sophisticated materials and techniques than more traditional folk art forms, it begins in precisely the same way: with imagination, scissors or knife, and paper.

Much van art is produced by professional craftsmen working for commercial factories and shops. One such craftsman is Steve Whatley of Baltimore, whose designs are suggested by the shape of the vehicle he is painting. Using lacquers and an air brush to achieve his effects, he proceeds in much the same way that individual van owners do to create their own effects, but with the special advantage of familiarity with automobile finishes. His advice for this section has been most valuable.

To create a stencil for a van painting, make a drawing on a large piece of thin cardboard or "Tufbak," a sticky-backed sheet material developed for the sign-painters trade. As you create the design, decide how many colors you will use and which portions of your design you will

Art on Wheels: Stencils for Van Painting

Van painting, "Tribute to Frazetti," by Steven Whatley, courtesy of Tower Ford, Inc.

devote to each. To make the next step easier, label the colors on your drawing.

After the surface of the van has been prepared in whatever way is recommended by the manufacturer of the finish being used, you are ready to begin the painting process. Tape your stencil to the van, making certain that it is properly aligned. If you use "Tufbak," simply peel off the backing a little at a time and press the stencil down against the van surface.

With a craft knife, cut away all of the areas that you have designated for a certain color. Make these cuts carefully and save the pieces. Then spray on the color. Follow the manufacturer's directions and try to avoid the sags and runs that result from a heavy hand on the spray gun. Lacquer dries quickly, and you will soon be able to replace those pieces you cut out, right over the dried paint. If necessary, use masking tape to hold the pieces in place and to seal any crevices.

Now proceed to cut away the areas for your second color, apply that color and, when it is dry, replace the cut-outs. Follow the same procedure for as many colors as you wish to apply.

An artist can carry this method to an amazing degree of detail and play endless variations on it. For example, Steve Whatley usually does the outlines and basic shapes by stenciling, then adds details and modeling with the airbrush used freehand. Sometimes he will cut a small stencil from cardboard and not even tape it to the surface—rather he will hand-hold it and move it about, developing his design as he goes along.

Once the artwork has been completed, it must be sealed with several coats of clear lacquer to protect it from the ravages of the weather and the open highway.

Printing Blocks

A paper-cutting can be used to good effect as a pattern for cutting a wooden or linoleum printing block. The paper from which the cutting is made should be of at least medium weight. The cut pattern will be fastened directly to the block. If you are using a wooden printing block, a water-soluble adhesive may be used, such as that on gummed-back craft paper. Since water-soluble adhesives will not stick to linoleum blocks, however, rubber cement can be used instead.

(A)

SUPPLIES:
PRINTING BLOCK (linoleum or wood)
PAPER (gummed-back, typing paper, gift wrap)
SCISSORS
PENCIL
WAXED PAPER
RUBBER CEMENT AND THINNER or
WATER-SOLUBLE PASTE

PROCEDURE:

1. On the paper you have selected, sketch your design or cut freehand, using any of the single-color flat-cut or fold-and-cut techniques described earlier in this book. I would suggest beginning with the simple two- or four-repeat patterns.

2. While making your pattern, you might allow the linoleum block to lie

in the hot sun and soften for a while. When warmed in this way the linoleum will cut like butter.

Now you are ready to mount your cutting onto the printing block. Using the technique below should minimize the amount of handling of the cutting.

(A) 1. Place the printing block on a piece of waxed paper and trace around it with a pencil.

2. Lay the waxed paper on a soft surface such as an ironing board or a piece of foam rug-padding.

(B) 3. Position the paper-cut pattern face down on the waxed-paper tracing of the block form. Secure it with a couple of straight pins if necessary.

(C)

4. Coat the pattern with adhesive—rubber cement for a linoleum block, paste for a wooden block or dampen with water if you are using gummed-back craft paper.

5. Remove the pins.

(C) 6. Carefully place the printing block face down on the cutting, making sure that it is aligned properly. Press down firmly without allowing the block to slip.

(D) 7. Now turn the entire "sandwich" over and slowly peel the waxed paper off. The cutting should remain firmly attached to the printing block.

8. Cover the cutting with a clean dry paper and rub vigorously from the center of the design to the edge to complete adhesion.

9. Allow the adhesive to dry before cutting the block.

10. Once the cutting of the block is completed, simply peel the pattern off, then rub the block gently with a rag dampened with water or rubber-cement thinner depending on the type of block you are using. Allow the block to dry before you use it for printing.

(D)

DON'T HURRY, AND DON'T FORGET TO SMELL THE FLOWERS

Paper-cutting by Joseph Koscinski. Courtesy of the artist

Children and Paper-Cutting

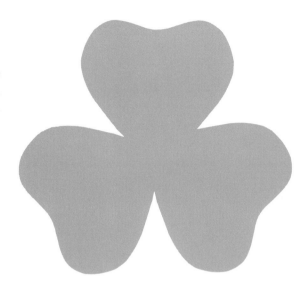

A three-leaf clover begins with the folding for a six-repeat pattern.

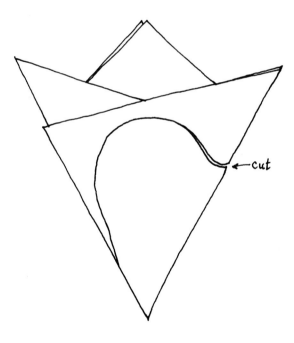

Children can become totally involved in paper-cutting from the time they are old enough to handle a blunt pair of scissors. In fact, the activity can be so intriguing that it will motivate them to learn to master the scissors. This, in turn, will help to develop the small muscles of the hand and wrist that are important in forming drawing and writing skills.

Of course, the young ones should be instructed first in scissors safety. They should be taught always to carry scissors—even blunt scissors—with the tapered end toward the floor. Children sometimes need reminding that scissors are for cutting, and not for pointing or thrusting at people.

I encourage parents and teachers to see that young children have a pair of scissors with smooth, comfortable handles and blades that move easily and are sharp enough to get the job done. Children trying to use a dull tool are just as likely to become frustrated as adults, and they become discouraged even more quickly.

In our house, we try to have a single place where scissors are kept when not in use. But since they never seem to stay there, they are identified by having different-colored handles, with each person—child and adult—responsible for having his own available any time it is wanted. And that system seems to work, because—as the children have found out—when you need a pair of scissors, you *need* a pair of *scissors!*

An adult who is going to interest or instruct children in paper-cutting must have mastered the technique himself first. I certainly don't mean that every adult interested in this art form has to be able to produce a full-color kodry style paper-cut picture. I do suggest that you try to master one or two procedures at a time so that when you show them to the children you appear confident in what you are doing. Your demonstration should convey the idea that paper-cutting is easy and enjoyable, and that even though it looks like magic, they can do it too!

Getting a feel for the materials is important. If you have collected some special papers for the project, let the children touch them and become familiar with them. The youngsters may well be fascinated by Oriental tea paper, origami paper, and papers having cotton as well as wood pulp in them. And they may delight in finding that some papers, good for cutting, come straight out of the old familiar waste-paper basket!

Of course, the age of the children will dictate how far they can be taken through the paper-cutting techniques. Nursery schoolers can do surprisingly competent and creative things with adult help. Older children with the dexterity to manage all of the folding and cutting techniques can be encouraged to do outstanding work on their own.

To start. My experience is that the best way to start is with a two-repeat design, so that the youngster does not become confused by multiple folds. Stick to a simple half-shape, such as half a heart or half a snowman. Cut out the shape, unfold the paper, and presto—there is the whole, perfectly balanced design!

The next step might be a four- or six-repeat design. For example, a simple, curving cut made in a square of paper folded for a six-repeat design will produce a three-leaf clover. Then go on to the folding for a ten-repeat design. Snip the paper only once, unfold it, and you have a five-pointed star.

Paper doll projects. Then, if your audience hasn't already deserted you in favor of scissors and paper, fold a long strip of paper to produce a border design or paper-doll series. Cut half a figure, making certain that some part of both folded edges remains intact. Unfold the paper once, and the half-figure has turned into a whole one. Unfold again, and the one has become two. Unfold for the final time and there are four figures holding hands. By this time, the children are usually thoroughly intrigued.

The paper-doll project can be tailored to fit either the season or the lesson at hand. For example, at Easter you can cut a spritely foursome of bunnies. Glue on cotton balls for tails, then turn the cutting over and add painted eyes and whiskers made from broom straws. Or, to make a history lesson more interesting, cut a series of dolls in the costume of the period you are studying. The ladies might be depicted with great bustles on the sides of their long dresses, while the men could wear top hats, long-tailed coats, and knee pants.

Historical flags. Paper-cutting lends itself nicely to a study of the history of the American flag. First, make certain that you have mastered the folding and cutting technique for a five-pointed star. Then, consult an encyclopedia or history text for illustrations of our national flags, beginning with the original thirteen-star flag adopted in 1777. I suggest using white paper as a base for all of the flags; a smaller piece of blue can be used for the field, and stripes can be cut from red. Almost all United States flag designs take seven red stripes. First add the field, then the stripes, and finally the five-pointed stars. Note that each star must be quite small, in no case larger than the width of a stripe. A compass or ruler might be helpful in making small, light pencil marks on the field to indicate where each star in the configuration is to be pasted.

Family crests. Once the children have mastered the basic fold-and-cut techniques, they are ready for a more ambitious project, such as an attempt to cut family crests in the Japanese manner. It would be well to have several examples of crests, illustrating how various identifying features are worked into the designs. Point out, for example, that a family that made its living by fishing might have a boat worked prominently into its crest, while military families often used arrows or other weapons in their designs. And some families chose designs simply because they were beautiful to look at, and these families had the sensitivity to enjoy beautiful things.

Youngsters can be encouraged to think about their own families. What do they enjoy doing as a family group? Camping? Swimming? Music? Photography? What articles or symbols from those activities could be worked into an attractive design?

Japanese family crests.

Children may enjoy illustrating their own stories with silhouettes cut from paper, in a style similar to this.

From Harriet Beecher Stowe, Connecticut Girl, *by Mabel Cleland, illustrated by Charles John, copyright© 1949 by the Bobbs-Merrill Co., Inc., reprinted with permission of the publisher*

Some children may prefer a more personal approach and want to cut a crest to identify themselves as individuals. If so, they should ask themselves what they enjoy doing, or how they think of themselves—as sports enthusiasts, readers, dancers, pet owners—or perhaps what they want to be when they grow up.

After each child has arrived at a crest with which to identify himself or his family, it can be cut numerous times, in different sizes if necessary, and glued proudly to his door, his lunch box, notebook and all manner of personal belongings.

Silhouettes. Children always enjoy the process of modeling for and making their own silhouettes. A child of nursery school or kindergarten age, even if too restless to pose, delights in having his entire figure modeled. To accomplish this, lay a large piece of brown wrapping paper on the floor. Have the child lie down on it with his arms away from his body and his legs slightly apart. Trace around him with a felt pen or pencil. Let the child cut out his silhouette and then paint or color in the hair, facial features and clothes. When it is finished, put it up on the wall and show it off.

Children who can sit still for a minute or two make good models for shadow silhouettes. Tape a large piece of newsprint or construction paper to a wall or flat perpendicular surface. Have the child sit on a chair in front of the paper with his side to it. Place a strong light so that it casts the shadow of the child's head onto the paper. Trace the shadow. Then let the child cut out his silhouette bust and glue it to another sheet of colored paper. You might even have him sign and date it as a record of just how he looked at that age.

Decoupage. After the children have mastered a few paper-cutting techniques, their collection of designs can be used for a simple decoupage project. A plain shoebox or ice cream carton can be decorated with favorite designs. First spray or paint the box or carton with two or three coats

Silhouettes

Decoupage

Kites

of enamel. The spraying should be done outside if possible and the children cautioned against standing downwind of the spray. When it is dry, lightly sand the surface with a fine-grained sandpaper and wipe it with a clean cloth.

Now have the child select the paper-cutting (or cuttings) to be used in the design. Spray both sides of it with a clear acrylic sealer and allow it to dry. Then place it face down on a piece of waxed paper. Using a soft brush and wallpaper paste or very thin glue, coat the back of the design. Pick up the waxed paper with the design on it and gently turn it onto the proper spot on the box or carton. Carefully press the design in place while it is still covered by the waxed paper. Gently peel the waxed paper off, and let the glue dry thoroughly. Now coat the entire surface of the box with varnish or shellac. Apply four or five coats, allowing each one to dry at least overnight before applying the next. An adult should be present during the varnishing process and it should be done in a well-ventilated area. To clean up after working with varnish, use turpentine; for cleaning up shellac, use alcohol. Finally, see that hands are washed with lots of strong soap and water.

The finished box will hold all kinds of personal treasures. A decoupaged ice cream carton makes a colorful waste basket or holder for magazines or sewing supplies.

Kites. Pretend-kites are fun to make and can be as simple or as complicated as the child's age and ability demand. Review with the youngster the procedure for a two-repeat design. Then help him select an appropriate form—a simple kite shape, a butterfly, bird, or even Batman. After the cutting is made (and decorated with colored paper shapes if desired), two holes should be punched about one inch apart in the center of the kite. Reinforce them with stick-on hole reinforcers from the dime-store. Pass a string through both holes, and tie it securely but not tightly. Let the child hold the strong and run, watching his very own "kite" flutter in the breeze behind him.

Applique. Making an appliqued pillow is not beyond the capability of many youngsters. The cut-paper pattern should be kept simple and used to cut the applique design from felt. Once the felt design is cut, it can be pinned or glued to the fabric square which is to become the pillow face. It can then be sewn on, by hand or machine, before the rest of the pillow is constructed. Remember, however, that felt is not washable.

Wall hangings. If an appliqued pillow seems too challenging, try a felt wall hanging. A host of interesting motifs, simple or complex, can be worked up from cut-paper patterns, transferred to felt pieces of various colors, and then glued or sewn to a background of felt or other suitable fabric.

Eggs. Easter eggs are ideal candidates for cut-paper designs. Whole eggs can be used if hard-boiled or, for more permanent art works, the shells alone can be decorated after the eggs have been blown out. Do this by carefully punching two holes, one in each end of a raw egg, with some kind of pointed instrument such as a skewer, a finishing nail or a knitting needle. Carefully break the yolk inside the egg by poking it with the pointed instrument. Hold the egg over a bowl and blow gently into the hole made in the top of the shell. The raw egg will come right out through the bottom hole, and can be saved for Easter morning breakfast. Rinse the shell thoroughly with water and allow it to dry.

Wall hangings

For decorating eggshells, encourage children to use gummed-back craft paper so that designs can be stuck to the delicate shells easily. Representational shapes such as hearts, flowers, birds or figures holding hands make attractive egg decorations, although the small scale necessitated by the size of the average egg makes them a bit challenging. For younger children, simple stripes or dots cut out with a paper punch and arranged in pleasing patterns are appropriate. In any case, some cut-paper design element should be positioned to cover each of the holes in the shell—unless a ribbon is to be strung through it so that the egg can be displayed on an Easter egg tree.

An Easter egg tree? Bring in a small branch from outside and set it upright by sticking it into a fairly large can filled with sand. The branch can be left plain, or spray-painted an attractive color. Decorate its branches with hanging Easter eggs. Pretty up the outside of that can of sand by wrapping it in paper to which cut-outs have been glued.

For children who are too young to handle eggshells, construction-paper egg shapes can be cut and decorated to their hearts' content with designs cut from colored tissue, gift wrap or more construction paper. With a hole punch and some string, these paper eggs can also be adapted for hanging.

Fantasy flowers. The Easter season, a time of rebirth and bloom, traditionally has lent itself to the creation of beautiful and imaginative floral designs from cut-paper. Children too can make compositions of brightly colored fantasy flowers. In fact, they can produce a three-dimensional

Eggs

Fantasy flowers

garden by fastening their cut-out blossoms to stems made of drinking straws. Fasten the blossoms to the straws with staples or a dab of white glue. Cut green leaves from paper to attach further down the stems. Insert the stems into shoe-box tops covered with green paper, onto which a stone can be glued to weight the "garden" down. Or display bouquets of imaginative flowers in juice cans filled with sand or plaster. Decorate the cans with other cut-out designs.

Masks. Children usually love to get involved in making their own costumes and masks for Halloween. Remember, of course, that costumes and candles are a dangerous combination, and that children should not carry or play near real jack-o-lanterns. With that precaution taken, let them make and wear the most outrageous costumes and masks imaginable.

Some may like to start with that old standby, the brown paper bag. Others may want to start from scratch by folding a stiff piece of paper once and cutting a basic mask-shape large enough to cover the face. Be sure that the eyes, nose and mouth are properly located, and that the eyeholes are large enough to allow eyelashes full room. Then turn the youngsters loose with some colored paper to decorate their masks. Show them how to fold the paper, right sides together, in order to cut shapes for both the right and left sides at the same time. Monster masks of a bilious green, bruise purple, blood red or sickening yellow paper are always great fun. Fasten all the colored decorations onto the basic mask with white glue. Then punch one hole on each side and strengthen each with hole-reinforcers from the dimestore. Tie yarn or twine through the holes and around behind the child's head to hold the mask on.

Some little girls may not admire the monster look, and masks with greater appeal—such as fairy-tale princess faces—must be made for them. The eyelashes should be long and gorgeous, the cheeks should be rosy pink spots, and the hair should flow in long curls under a princess crown or tall hat—all cut from paper and glued in place on the cut-paper mask.

Christmas. In the earlier section on adult Christmas decorations (pages 70-72) there are several suggestions for creations children can make. Since at Christmas, more than any other time, paper-cutting tends to become a family affair, let this hobby really shine throughout the holidays. And to

94

Masks

demonstrate your "togetherness" to all visitors, try this: Cut a large Christmas tree from a piece of paper folded once. Put it up on a wall, door or bulletin board, and let everyone decorate it with his or her own fold-and-cut paper designs. See if your family and friends can completely cover the tree form. It will look as though it is made out of lace!

A Lowicz-style medallion by the author.

Expanding Your Horizons

By now we know that paper-cutting is a many-faceted art form. It can be a simple means of self-expression—something to be picked up and done for the sheer joy of a creative encounter between paper, scissors and imagination. Or it can be an involved and complex medium, requiring painstaking care and challenging the skill of any artist.

Almost as old as paper itself, paper-cutting remains so universally accessible and appealing that the various adaptations of the art form discussed here are sure to lead to even more possibilities for the future. For instance, the commercial applications of paper-cut design in such areas as book illustration, advertising and packaging are for the most part still unexplored.

Because paper-cutting can accommodate itself to nearly any level of proficiency, it is an activity in which the entire family can share. As such, it can become an effective way to relive—and revive—a family's ethnic heritage. The art form provides a visual and tactile means of awakening in children an awareness of their cultural background. Nor are young people the only ones with whom your acquired knowledge and experience can be shared. Paper-cutting provides a marvelous opportunity to enrich the lives of retired, elderly or institutionalized people. Even those whose physical abilities are impaired can master the techniques necessary to produce fulfilling and creative work in paper. How satisfying it can be to a senior citizen today to discover an art form in which he or she is able not only to compete with younger folk, but perhaps surpass them!

The art form is not only a creative medium for the practitioner but an exciting and relatively untapped field for the collector. To be sure, the classic designs of Edouart, von Gunten and others have already appeared sporadically in collections. But still waiting to be discovered are countless anonymous examples of every folk culture. The key is selectivity; the collector's choices today may well become the valued—and valuable—classics of the future, in much the same way that today's museums cherish the anonymous valentines of the Pennsylvania Dutch of a century ago.

Antique and second-hand shops, museum shops, flea markets and craft shows in every part of the world are all fertile avenues to explore. When in quest of antique work, however, be careful to distinguish between hand work and what evidently were mass-produced commodities stamped out around the turn of the century. These latter pieces can sometimes be identified by the sophistication of their design; in any case, an examination of the underside of the cutting (if you are permitted to

The serious collector should be able to recognize stamped-out cuttings. Collection of Stemmer House Publishers, Inc.

Courtesy of Carol Lynch Perry

remove it from its frame) will tell the story. If the paper has been stamped rather than cut, the reverse side of the perforations will have raised edges as easy to see and feel as those on the undersides of today's paper doilies. Not that mass-produced cuttings are to be scorned—many of these elaborate confections are delightfully nostalgic. However, as a serious collector you will want to develop the ability to recognize them.

Contemporary ethnic work, imported from its homeland, can form the basis of an interesting and potentially valuable collection. It can sometimes be found in stores specializing in imported goods, such as Chinese, Japanese, Mexican and Polish shops. A partial list of these can be found in the source list in the Appendix.

Displayed singly or in groupings, paper cuttings make handsome interior wall designs. You and your family and guests will find it fascinating to examine and compare the materials and techniques used, especially once you have practiced the art form yourself. You may decide to limit your acquisitions to a single type of cutting or to a single cultural tradition, or you may delight in acquiring examples of every variety discussed in this book, together with contemporary adaptations of the techniques. Either way, a surprisingly modest investment can bring a great deal of beauty and pleasure.

To broaden your knowledge of classic design, you might begin looking for examples of paper-cut designs in the museums in your area and in those encountered while traveling. Probably you will find few, if any, on display. But by asking the museum librarian, you may find—and be permitted to view—examples "hidden" in the collection, thus heightening your own sense of discovery. Ultimately, your interest may kindle that of the museum staff and even result in an exhibition combining the museum's paper-cutting treasures with yours and those of other collectors. And from there, who knows what acquisitions and inspirations may follow! In 1976, New York City's Museum of Modern Art traded almost one million dollars' worth of works in its collections for a paper-cut work by Henri Matisse, who in his last years turned to this medium. Matisse found it to be an art form well-suited to his declining physical abilities but still sharp artistic sense.

Henri Matisse, Memory of Oceania, 1953. *gouache and crayon on cut-and-pasted paper on canvas, 9'4" x 9'4⅞". Collection, The Museum of Modern Art, New York. Mrs. Simon Guggenheim Fund*

A previous acquisition by the same artist, *Memory of Oceania*, is described thus:

> The *Memory of Oceania*, one of the most abstract compositions that Matisse ever created, is not a portrayal of a tropical paradise so much as an evocation of his pleasurable, sensuous recollections of a visit to Tahiti made twenty-three years earlier. . . .
> This huge composition, over nine feet square, was produced by Matisse at the age of eighty-four. In ill health, and confined to

his bed or a wheelchair, he refused to allow infirmity to hamper his exhuberant creativity. Unable to work at an easel, he developed on a monumental scale a medium with which he had first experimented in 1931. From sheets of paper painted with gouache in colors of his choosing, he cut out forms with a scissors and arranged them on a background. In the *Memory of Oceania*, he also used a black crayon to draw a few lines that magically conjure up the image of a reclining nude.

The orange border surrounding the picture is intercepted at intervals by bars of black. Within this frame, rectangles of differing proportions are combined with irregular shapes. The various forms in two shades of yellow, bright orange, its complementary blue, leaf green, magenta and black are overlaid upon one another and set against the open white field with its crayon drawing. The prevailing impression of the composition, despite the flatness of all its elements, is one of airiness and space.

"There is no break between my painting and my cut-outs," Matisse said. *"Only, with something more of the abstract and the absolute, I have arrived at a distillation of form. . . . Of this or that object which I used to present in all its complexity in space, I now keep only the sign, which suffices . . . for the composition as I conceive it."*

Henri Matisse, heir to an art form more than a thousand years old, has left with us brilliant demonstrations of how far paper-cutting may take a creative mind.

Sources of Materials

ART THINGS, INC.
2 Annapolis Street
W. Annapolis, Maryland 21401
Tea chest paper, all types of decoupage supplies

ANDREWS/NELSON/WHITEHEAD
31-10 48 Avenue
Long Island City, New York 11101
Imported papers

CHINESE BOOKS AND PERIODICALS
125 Fifth Avenue
New York, New York 10010
Books, woodblock prints, greeting cards and other
Chinese imports

CEPELIA CORPORATION
236 Fifth Avenue
New York, New York 10010
Polish imports

DENNISON MANUFACTURING COMPANY
Framingham, Massachusetts 01701
Papers, including gift wrap and
gummed-back craft paper

THE HOUSE OF JAPANESE PRODUCTS
1522 York Road
Lutherville, Maryland 21093
Japanese imports, including books on Japanese arts,
origami paper

LeeWards Creative Crafts Center
1200 St. Charles Road
Elgin, Illinois 60120
Decoupage materials, scissors and other craft supplies

THE OLD WARSAW DELICATESSEN
1737 Fleet Street
Baltimore, Maryland 21231
Wycinanki paper and Polish imports

PANDA HOUSE
7842 Wisconsin Avenue
Bethesda, Maryland 20014
Chinese imports, including paper-cuttings

TAKASHIMAYA
509 Fifth Avenue
New York, New York 10017
Origami paper and Japanese imports

Bibliography

AN INVITATION TO SEE: 125 PAINTINGS FROM THE MUSEUM OF MODERN ART by Helen M. Franc. New York: The Museum of Modern Art, 1973.

CHINESE FOLK DESIGNS, by W. M. Hawley. New York: Dover Publications, Inc., 1971.

CHINESE PAPER CUTOUTS, by J. Hejzlar. London: Spring House, n.d.

CHINESE PAPER-CUT PICTURES, Old and Modern, by Nancy Kuo. London: Alec Tiranti, 1964.

DESIGN AND PAPER XIV. New York: Marquardt and Company, Inc. n.d.

INDEX OF AMERICAN DESIGN, by Erwin O. Christensen. New York: The Macmillan Company, 1950.

JAPANESE DESIGN MOTIFS, translated by Fumie Adachi. New York: Dover Publications, Inc., 1972 .

MON-KIRI, by Isao Honda. San Francisco: Japan Publications, Inc., 1972.

PAPER AS ART AND CRAFT, by Thelma R. Newman, Jay Hartley Newman and Lee Scott Newman. New York: Crown Publishers, Inc., 1973.

PAPER CUTTING, by Florence Temko. Garden City: Doubleday and Company, Inc., 1973.

PENNSYLVANIA DUTCH AMERICAN FOLK ART, by Henry J. Kauffman. New York: Dover Publications, Inc., 1964.

SCHERENSCHNITTE, THE FOLK ART OF SCISSORS CUTTING, by Claudia Hopf. Lancaster, Pennsylvania: John Baer's Sons, 1971.

SHADES OF OUR ANCESTORS, AMERICAN PROFILES AND PROFILISTS, by Alice Van Leer Carrick. Boston: Little, Brown, and Company, 1928.

THE ART OF PAPER TEARING, by Eric Hawkesworth. London: Faber and Faber, 1973.

THE FLOWERING OF AMERICAN FOLK ART 1776-1876, by Jean Lipman and Alice Winchester. New York: The Viking Press, in cooperation with the Whitney Museum of American Art, 1974.

THE HISTORY OF SILHOUETTES, by E. Nevill Jackson. London: The Connoisseur, 1911.

WYCINANKI, POLISH FOLK PAPER-CUTS, compiled by Anna Zejac Gacek. New Bedford, Massachusetts: Sarmatia Publications, 1972.